The Teen's
Vegetarian
Cookbook

by Judy Krizmanic
Illustrations by Matthew Wawiorka

VIKING

For Mero Sahti and for Aiko

VIKING
Published by the Penguin Group
Penguin Putnam Books for Young Readers, 345 Hudson Street,
New York, New York 10014, U.S.A.
Penguin Books Ltd, 27 Wrights Lane, London W8 5TZ, England
Penguin Books Australia Ltd, Ringwood, Victoria, Australia
Penguin Books Canada Ltd, 10 Alcorn Avenue, Toronto, Ontario, Canada M4V 3B2
Penguin Books (N.Z.) Ltd, 182-190 Wairau Road, Auckland 10, New Zealand

Penguin Books Ltd, Registered Offices: Harmondsworth, Middlesex, England

Published by Viking and Puffin Books,
members of Penguin Putnam Books for Young Readers, 1999

3 5 7 9 10 8 6 4 2

LIBRARY OF CONGRESS CATALOGING-IN-PUBLICATION DATA
Krizmanic, Judy.
The teen's vegetarian cookbook / by Judy Krizmanic ;
illustrations by Matthew Wawiorka.
p. cm.
Includes Index.
Summary: Recipes for all types of vegetarian dishes are
accompanied by information and advice on vegetarian diet and quotes
from teenage vegetarians.
ISBN 0-670-87426-4 (hardcover). —ISBN 0-14-038506-1 (pbk.)
1. Vegetarian cookery—Juvenile literature. [1. Vegetarian
cookery.] I. Wawiorka, Matthew, ill. II. Title.
TX837.K75 1999 641.5'636—dc21 98-21856 CIP AC

Printed in the United States of America
Set in Minion

Publisher's Note
**The ideas and information contained in this book are not intended
as a substitute for consulting with a physician. All matters regarding
health require medical supervision.**

Acknowledgments

They say that too many cooks spoil the broth, but I say many cooks and friends make a project more fun. Hearty thanks to all who contributed to this one.

To all the teens who generously shared ideas, experiences, and recipes. Your insights are what will make this book special to those who use it.

To friends who gave recipes, to those who tasted, and to those who ate the leftovers.

To Carol Coughlin, R.D., for contributing nutrition information, recipes, food tips, the substitution chart, and her trademark enthusiasm.

To Deborah Brodie of Viking Children's Books, whose perseverance and generous sprinkling of culinary (and editorial) wisdom guided this project.

To Judy Carey and Janet Pascal, who worked hard to make this happen.

To Peggy Guthart for all of her support and great ideas—and for getting the word out.

To Lisa Bernstein for providing the spark.

To my family for giving recipes and tons of encouragement through the busiest year I've known.

To my husband, Bill Weingarten—the most thanks. I still maintain you are the best cook in our house. Your inspiration, support, and channa masala will ever astound me.

To Sahti.

And to BD.

Contents

GET COOKING!

" *Cooking is more about having fun than following a recipe to the letter.* **"** —**Tex, 15**

Welcome to the world of vegetarian cooking! Since I wrote my first book, *A Teen's Guide to Going Vegetarian,* lots of people have asked me, "What advice do you give to teens who are just starting out as vegetarians?" One thing that I always suggest is that you get in the kitchen, roll up your sleeves, and cook.

Why cook? For one thing, cooking will make your menu much more exciting. Sure, you could eat around the meat that your family is eat-

> For information on vegetarian foods and cooking terms, turn to the glossary on page 171.

ing, but side dishes can get pretty boring after a while.

Cooking for yourself can earn you a little respect. When you learn how to make a few things for yourself, your family will notice that you're taking responsibility for your decision to go vegetarian. Most parents are really glad when their vegetarian kids learn how to cook, partly because they're not sure what to make for you anyway.

Also, cooking is an act of independence. You call the shots. When you're making dinner, you can put in the ingredients that *you* like.

At the same time, cooking connects you with other people—even people who eat differently from you. You can make anything in this book and share it with your family and friends. Meatless food isn't just for vegetarians.

But maybe the most con-

A Word about Vegetables

I know some people who say they don't like vegetables. Then I find out why. They grew up with vegetables that were always overcooked and served in a bland little pile of mush on the side of the plate, or completely drowned in butter. (What if I told a meat eater that I didn't like meat, and then confessed that the only way that I had ever had it was burnt to a crisp?)

vincing reason to start cooking is that cooking is fun! It's relax-ing! It's a great feeling to put on your favorite music, chop up a bunch of veggies, and see what you can come up with.

Some General Cooking Tips

1. *Be patient.* Don't feel like you have to become a cooking wizard overnight. Try mastering a few fast-and-easy dishes first. Use this cookbook to find your cooking comfort level. Some of the recipes in this book are super fast and easy (look for the "Insanely Easy" icon). Others require more chopping or longer cooking. But nothing in this book is terribly difficult.

And think about how to build upon basic things that you already know how to make. "Some quick meals are stir-fry with tofu, pasta with sauce and veggies, and baked potatoes with veggies and pasta sauce," says Mara, 17.

Remember, cooking skills improve over time, says Christina, 14. "I'm getting better at chopping stuff. When you watch the cooking shows, they're just slicing and dicing like crazy. It used to take me 15 minutes to chop an onion."

2. *Don't worry about making mistakes.* Cooking is all about trial and error. "Once I cooked myself tofu burgers, but I had only the very soft kind of tofu," says Erin, 16. "When I finished it, it was so runny it could not be put into a burger, much less into my mouth. The worst part was that I had misread the servings, and I had made enough for six people. It was really bad!"

At the same time, you'll soon discover that most "disasters" are actually quite fixable.

insanely**easy**

Look for the Insanely Easy Icon

Most of the recipes in this book are pretty easy, but the ones marked with this icon are especially so. Insanely Easy recipes meet at least two of the following criteria:
- *use few ingredients*
- *involve little or no chopping or other preparation*
- *require minimal cooking time*

In fact, that's how some new dishes get created. For example, the Nacho Cheeseless Sauce in this book (page 43) was created when I was trying to make a tofu omelet. I realized it looked more like cheese sauce, so I took the recipe in an entirely different direction.

Did You Know?
About 25 percent of teenagers say being a vegetarian is "in" according to Teenage Research Unlimited, a marketing research firm specializing in teens.

3. *Give yourself enough time.* People often ask me, "Does vegetarian food take longer to prepare?" Longer than what? I find it pretty amazing that people think it's normal to take the time to clean a whole chicken and then wait for the thing to roast in the oven. Plan ahead so you have what you need and are sure you have time to complete the recipe. But remember: before you turn the page on a recipe because the ingredient list looks long, give it a closer look. In most cases, many of the ingredients are spices and things that require no chopping, just a quick toss into the pot.

4. *Experiment with new foods.* Don't feel like

Where Do You Find the Ingredients?

Most of the ingredients in this book are things you can find in any supermarket. Actually, it's getting easier all the time to find vegetarian-friendly ingredients just about anywhere.

A handful of recipes in this book do call for things that you can only find in the natural foods store or other specialty store. These are not foods that you must eat in order to be a vegetarian, but they do add variety and nutrients. "If there's a natural foods store near you, I think you should check it out," says vegetarian teen Jason F. "I know the first few times I went, I was astounded by all the specialty items and products specifically for vegetarians. I wanted to try them all."

Other good places to shop include ethnic groceries, farmers markets, and mail order sources listed at the back of some vegetarian magazines. Hint: If you want your parents to buy an unusual ingredient, it helps to show them a recipe you're planning to use so they know it won't go to waste.

you have to get a handle on every plant food ever grown in order to be a vegetarian or a vegetarian cook. Just try a new vegetable, bean, or grain every now and then. If you don't like something, move on to something else. It's that simple.

5. *Use recipes as an inspiration, not as a set of rules.* Add your favorite spices and vegetables to recipes, and leave out the ones you don't like. "I've found that cooking is more about having fun than following a recipe to the letter," says Tex, 15. Taste your food while you're cooking it, and adjust seasonings as you go along. "Be experimental, and do not fear the kitchen," advises Maureen, 18. "It's your friend!"

Holiday Ideas

What do you eat when the rest of the family is gobbling up Thanksgiving turkey or other holiday dishes? Try a no-fuss yet festive recipe like Annie's Easy Risotto (page 69), Vegetable Couscous Marinara (page 70) or Savory Roasted Seitan (page 57) with Easy Veggie Gravy (page 58). Serve with all the wonderful vegetable dishes that go with the holidays.

Make Your Own Veggie Stuffing: *Most holiday cooks use turkey broth to make their stuffing. Ask your family chef to leave some stuffing plain and then use vegetable broth to make yours. Aside from the turkey, gravy, and stuffing, most other Thanksgiving and holiday foods are vegetarian-friendly.*

Stuff a Squash: *Bake some acorn or delicata squash according to directions on pages 140–41, and stuff with vegetarian stuffing dressed up with chopped walnuts, apples, and raisins. Bake at 350°F for about 20 minutes.*

Finish with a Flourish: *Make Sweet Potato Pumpkin Pie (page 157–58) or Baked Pears with Spiced Orange Sauce (page 155) for the whole family.*

The How-To-Get-Your-Nutrients Substitution Chart

There's no one food that you have to eat, but there are nutrients you have to get. This chart will help you get what you need without having to choke down foods you don't like. It was created by my friend Carol Coughlin, a registered dietitian, who advises vegetarian teens around the country.

You gotta have:	If you don't like:	Try:	Then try:
Calcium	Milk or calcium-fortified soymilk	Calcium-fortified rice milk or juices (orange, apple, cranberry); greens (kale, collard, mustard greens, turnip greens); broccoli; tahini (sesame paste); figs; almonds; tofu made with calcium (read label); blackstrap molasses; yogurt or cheese.	Calcium supplements (you can mix powdered calcium supplements or powdered soymilk into baked goods and pancakes).
Protein	Beans or tofu	Hide beans by mashing them and adding them to soups. Use refried beans or hummus as a spread instead of mayo or mustard. Crumble tofu into spaghetti sauce.	Other high protein foods, such as soy based veggie burgers, dogs, and other "fake meat"; seitan; soymilk; nut butters; high protein grains (such as millet, quinoa, amaranth, and buckwheat).

You gotta have:	If you don't like:	Try:	Then try:
Fiber and trace minerals	Whole grains	Use a mixture of white and whole wheat flour when making baked goods.	Lots of fruits and veggies for fiber; nuts for trace minerals.
		Try a new recipe. Your usual spaghetti sauce may taste weird with whole wheat spaghetti, but if you try a whole new sauce, you won't be comparing it to the old dish.	
Iron	Dark green leafy vegetables	Don't just steam the greens; finely chop them and add a little to a favorite dish, like a stir-fry.	Other iron-rich foods, like lentils and other cooked beans; seitan; dried fruits (raisins, apricots, figs).
Vitamin C	Fresh fruit	Use orange juice or strawberry juice as part of the liquid in pancake batter; freeze fruit and juice into fruit pops.	Green peppers; potatoes; hot peppers.
Vitamin A	Vegetables	See "10 Ways to Love Vegetables" (page 145).	Red grapefruit; oranges.

You gotta have:	If you don't like:	Try:	Then try:
Vitamin B$_{12}$	Dairy products or eggs	Fortified soymilk or rice milk; fortified breakfast cereals; Red Star Nutritional Yeast Vegetarian Support Formula, T6635.	Take a B$_{12}$ supplement if you don't consume B$_{12}$ fortified foods regularly.
Folate (a.k.a. folic acid or folacin)	Green leafy veggies	Hide green veggies in recipes you like; drink orange juice; eat fortified grain foods and cereals.	Oranges, peanuts, sunflower seeds.
Riboflavin (vitamin B$_2$)	Dairy products	Fortified soy milk and fortified cereals.	Broccoli, asparagus, turnip greens, spinach.
Magnesium	Whole grains	Beans such as black beans and navy beans, nuts, seeds.	Green vegetables, avocados, berries, chocolate (really! But don't overdo it. . . .).
Zinc	Whole grains or hard cheeses*	Legumes (beans); almonds and other nuts; avocados.	Fake meats that have zinc added.

* If you get your zinc from whole grains, you should know that your body can absorb more zinc from foods made with yeast (e.g., breads rather than muffins) and from sprouted grains.

For more nutrition information, read: A Teen's Guide to Going Vegetarian by Judy Krizmanic (Viking and Puffin Books). Good News About Good Food by Carol M. Coughlin, R.D. (Cucurbita Moschata Publishing, 191 Baldwin Street, Leicester, MA 01524).

Get Your Calcium and Iron
Good Calcium Sources

If you don't eat dairy products (and even if you do), add these calcium-rich foods to your diet. If you're not getting the recommended calcium amount from food (1300 mg./day for teens), take a supplement.

Calcium-fortified orange juice, 8 ounces: 300 mg.
Calcium-fortified soymilk, 8 ounces: 200 mg.–500 mg.
   (depends on brand)
Calcium-fortified rice milk, 8 ounces: 240 mg.
Collard greens, 1 cup cooked: 145 mg.
Bok choy, 1 cup cooked: 158 mg.
Broccoli, 1 cup cooked: 178 mg.
Okra, 1 cup cooked: 100 mg.
Tempeh, 1 cup: 170 mg.
Tofu (firm, processed with calcium sulfate), 4 ounces:
   250 mg.–350 mg.
Navy beans, 1 cup cooked: 128 mg.
Pinto beans, 1 cup cooked: 90 mg.
Figs, 5 medium: 135 mg.
Blackstrap molasses, 2 Tablespoons: 274 mg.
Tahini (sesame butter), 2 Tablespoons: 128 mg.

Good Iron Sources

Meat is not the only source of iron. Eat these iron-rich plant foods with a vitamin C–rich food (like orange juice or tomatoes), to help your body absorb the iron.

Chard, 1 cup cooked: 4.0 mg.
Spinach, 1 cup cooked: 3.2 mg.
Lentils, 1 cup cooked: 6.6 mg.
Pinto beans, 1 cup cooked: 6.8 mg.
Blackstrap molasses, 2 Tablespoons: 6.4 mg.
Chickpeas, 1 cup cooked: 4.7 mg.
Seitan, 4 ounces: 4.0 mg.
Potato, 1 medium: 2.8 mg.
Tofu, 4 ounces: 1.0 mg.–11 mg.
Apricots, dried, 10 halves: 1.7 mg.

BREAKFAST

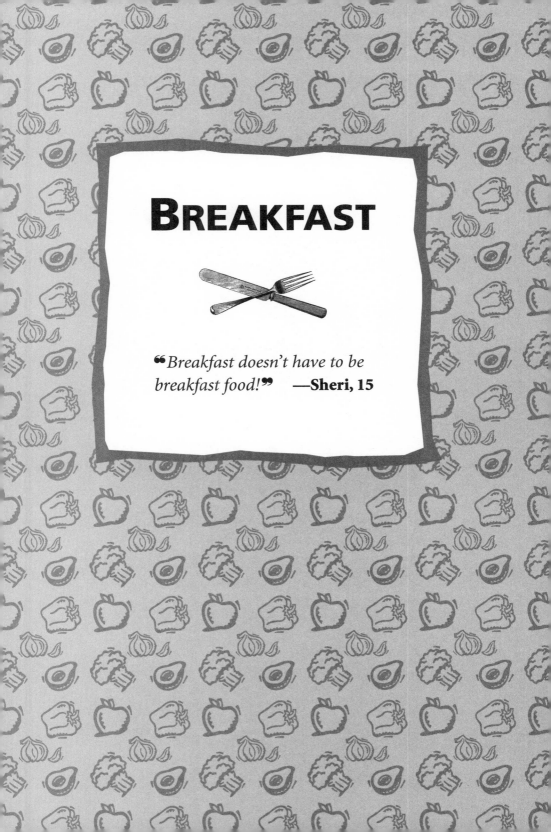

❝Breakfast doesn't have to be breakfast food!❞ —**Sheri, 15**

Everyone knows that breakfast is important, but we're talking about a time of day when you're either in a rush or half asleep. It's easy to get stuck in the old corn flakes routine. How do you break out of breakfast boredom? This section contains recipes and ideas for busy days as well as days when you have more time to experiment.

Easy Homemade Granola

This is adapted from a favorite recipe of Julia, a 14-year-old vegan. Feel free to adjust amounts to get the sweetness and texture you like best.

1 cup sunflower seeds (hulls removed)
½ cup sesame seeds
¼ cup almonds (chopped or slivered)
3 cups rolled oats
¼ cup flour
½ cup brown sugar or apple juice
    concentrate, mixed with ½ cup water
5 Tablespoons vegetable oil
½ teaspoon salt
1 Tablespoon vanilla
3 to 4 Tablespoons
    natural maple syrup
1 teaspoon cinnamon
½ cup dried fruit, such as
    raisins, apricot pieces,
    cherries, or cranberries

1. Preheat oven to 350° F.
2. In a skillet containing no oil or liquid, combine the seeds and nuts. Heat over a low

> ### insanely**easy**
> #### Creative Breakfast Bagels
> **Nutty Banana Spice Bagel:** *Combine* **1 Tablespoon peanut butter** *with* ½ **mashed banana** *and a dash of* **cinnamon**. *Spread on a* **toasted bagel** *(cinnamon raisin tastes good).*
>
> **Italian Basil Bagel:** *Spread a* **toasted bagel** *(sesame, herb, or pumpernickel is tasty) with* **tofu mayonnaise** *(recipe, page 28) and top with* **fresh basil leaves** *and* **tomato slices**.

insanely**easy**

Instant Banana Breakfast Sauce

Here's a fast topping for granola, cereal, or even toast: In a blender, combine 1 **banana, 1 Tablespoon raspberry or strawberry preserves,** *and* ⅓ **cup drained silken tofu.** *Blend until smooth.*

flame, stirring frequently, just until you start smelling a toasty, warm aroma. (Keep watching and don't let them burn.) You can also toast them for 2 minutes in a pan in a toaster oven set on a low setting.

3. In a large bowl, combine toasted seeds and nuts with remaining ingredients, except dried fruit. Spread the mixture onto 2 cookie sheets and bake for about 20 minutes, or until golden, turning the mixture frequently with a spatula or wooden spoon while baking. Remove from oven and leave granola on pan while cooling. Add dried fruit to granola and stir to combine. Store in an airtight container. Makes about 6 cups.

Variation: For a different flavor, experiment with different **nuts,** or add a touch of **orange or maple extract** to the granola. Also, adjust the sweetness to your liking by adding or reducing brown sugar, apple juice concentrate, or maple syrup.

insanely**easy**

Berry Breakfast Shake

> 5 ice cubes
> 1 cup frozen or fresh mixed berries
> 1 ripe banana
> ½ cup silken tofu (to make this shake extra creamy and give protein)
> ¾ cup orange juice or soymilk

1. Crush the ice cubes in a blender.
2. Add berries and "pulse" the blender until berries are pureed. Add remaining ingredients and puree until smooth. Makes one big shake.

Variations: Experiment with different kinds of fruits (try **mangoes, blueberries, peaches,** or **strawberries**) and juices (**pineapple** and **apple** are good).

insanelyeasy

Orange Wake-up Smoothie

5 ice cubes
3 Tablespoons frozen orange juice concentrate
1 banana
½ cup soymilk
¼ cup pineapple juice (or use extra soymilk
  instead)
2 Tablespoons silken tofu (optional, but it
  adds creaminess)

1. Crush the ice cubes in a blender.
2. Add remaining ingredients and blend until creamy. Makes
one big smoothie.

What Is a Vegetarian?

*By definition, a vegetarian is a person who doesn't eat any meat—
that means no beef, no pork, no poultry, and no fish. You'll soon
realize, though, that people use the word pretty loosely. Some people
who eat fish call themselves vegetarian. Some people who eat chick-
en call themselves vegetarian, too. It's good to be accepting of people
as they explore a change in diet. It's also good to have a definition,
so that people know what you're talking about. What do you think
the definition of* vegetarian *should be?*

Dairy-free French Toast

*Soymilk and applesauce replace the milk and eggs usually found
in French toast batter.*

½ cup fortified soymilk
½ cup applesauce (or try 1 mashed banana
  instead)
2 Tablespoons vegetable oil
1 Tablespoon flour
Pinch of salt

Dash of cinnamon

4 slices dairy-free whole wheat bread

1. In a bowl, mix together soymilk, applesauce, and 1 Tablespoon of the oil. Add flour, salt, and cinnamon to make batter.

2. Heat a nonstick griddle or frying pan over medium high flame until a few drops of water drizzled onto it forms beads and bounces around. Pour remaining oil onto the griddle and heat until hot.

3. When oiled griddle is hot, quickly dip two bread slices into batter, lightly coating both sides. Place bread slices on hot griddle and cook for 1 or 2 minutes on one side, flip with spatula, and cook on opposite side for another minute or 2. Continue cooking, flipping occasionally, until both sides are browned, about 5 minutes in all.

> **Banana Crunch To Go**
>
> *Take a **banana** and a plastic baggie of **cereal** with you. On your way to school, peel the banana and dunk it in the dry cereal, which will stick to the banana. Re-dunk before each bite.*

4. Add more oil to griddle, if necessary, and repeat with any remaining bread. Serve French toast with maple syrup, organic yogurt, or sprinkle with powdered sugar. Makes 4 slices.

Sweet hint: Use vanilla soymilk or rice milk instead of the plain kind in French toast and pancakes for extra flavor.

Vegan Pancakes

½ cup whole wheat flour

½ cup unbleached white flour

1 Tablespoon baking powder

¼ teaspoon salt

1 cup soymilk, rice milk, or dairy milk

2½ Tablespoons vegetable oil

2 Tablespoons liquid sweetener, such as maple syrup, apple juice concentrate, barley malt, rice syrup, or honey

1. Combine flours, baking powder, and salt in a bowl. Combine milk, 2 Tablespoons of the oil, and sweetener in a separate bowl.

2. Add milk mixture to flour mixture and mix just until moistened; a few lumps are okay. (Don't overbeat, or pancakes will be tough.)

3. Heat a nonstick griddle or frying pan over medium high flame until a few drops of water drizzled onto it forms beads and bounces around. Pour remaining ½ Tablespoon of oil onto the griddle and heat until hot.

4. Pour batter onto the griddle to form circles about 4 inches in diameter. Cook the pancakes for a minute or 2 on one side. When bubbles appear on the surface, slide a spatula under the pancake and flip it over. Cook the pancakes on the other side for another 1 or 2 minutes. Continue to cook the pancakes, occasionally flipping them until golden brown on each side, about 4 minutes in all. When finished, remove from skil-

---

What's the Deal with Dairy?

Some vegetarians eat dairy products. Others don't. Teens who go vegan say that even though cows aren't killed during milk production, they don't want to support any industry that confines animals for human use. In confinement, dairy cows are forced to produce many times more milk that they would naturally (sometimes through the use of hormones). And often in the end, dairy cows are eventually slaughtered for meat.

If you don't want to use dairy products, it's easy to cook without them. You'll notice in this cookbook that whenever milk or cheese or yogurt is listed in a recipe, the non-dairy version of that ingredient is listed first. (You can find soymilk, rice milk, soy margarine, and other non-dairy foods in natural foods stores and in many supermarkets. Make sure to buy the calcium-fortified versions of these foods, especially if you don't eat any dairy products at all.) If you like dairy products, feel free to use them in these recipes. The choice is up to you.

let and put on serving plate. Repeat with remaining batter. Makes about 8 pancakes.

Variations: Try adding a handful of fresh **blueberries,** chopped **peaches or apples, raisins, walnuts, pecans, or chocolate chips** to your pancakes. A dash of **cinnamon** in the batter is nice, too.

---

insanelyeasy

Ridiculously Quick Breakfast Ideas

"I'm usually rushed in the morning because I oversleep a lot,"
admits Sheri, 15. If you're someone who hits "snooze" five times,
try snagging one of these for breakfast:
  Toasted bread with peanut butter and cinnamon
  Bagel with peanut butter and jelly
  Banana soymilk fruit juice smoothie
  Instant breakfast-in-a-cup meals (found in natural foods stores
    and some groceries)
  Instant oatmeal with cut-up fresh fruit
  Soy yogurt or dairy yogurt with wheat germ or cereal sprinkled on top
  Muffin with peanut butter or tahini (see muffin recipe, page 23)
  Cereal topped with fruit, nuts, and soymilk
  Leftover veggie pizza or other leftovers

Breakfast Scrambler

"Instead of scrambled eggs, try scrambled tofu," says Jason G., 19.
"You can also add garlic, chili powder, or whatever sounds good."
Try serving it with fake sausage or bacon, available at natural
foods stores.

  16 ounce package firm or extra-firm tofu, drained
  2 Tablespoons vegetable oil
  ½ medium onion, finely chopped, or
      3 scallions (also called green onions),
      cut into small pieces
  1 clove garlic, peeled and finely chopped
  ½ teaspoon turmeric
  ½ teaspoon cumin (optional)

2 teaspoons tamari or soy sauce
Pepper to taste
Sesame seeds for sprinkling

1. Press water out of tofu by wrapping a paper towel or a clean dish towel around the tofu block, holding it over the sink and squeezing. (See "Tofu Tips," page 176.) Set tofu aside.
2. Heat oil in a skillet. Add onion and sauté for 2 minutes. Add garlic and sauté 1 more minute, but don't let garlic turn brown.
3. Crumble the tofu into onion-garlic mixture and stir. Add turmeric and cumin and sauté for about 4 minutes, stirring occasionally until tofu is thoroughly heated. Add tamari or soy sauce and sauté for 1 more minute.
4. Sprinkle with sesame seeds. Serve with whole wheat toast. Serves 2 to 4.

Variation: To make **Scrambled Tofu with Veggies,** add 1½ **cups finely chopped veggies** after the tofu has been cooking for a few minutes. Continue cooking, covered, for 3 or 4 more minutes, until veggies are cooked. Use any combination of vegetables, such as **zucchini, broccoli, mushrooms, green pepper, carrots,** or **yellow crookneck squash.**

Hint: Do you like **ketchup** with your scrambled eggs? It's good with scrambled tofu, too.

Salsa Scramble
Tortilla chips add a nice surprise to this dish, which is great for brunch. Serve with leftover brown rice or black beans on the side.

2 Tablespoons vegetable oil
½ medium onion, thinly sliced
8 ounces firm tofu, drained, pressed (see page 176), and cut into 1-inch cubes
2 cups corn tortilla chips
1½ cups bottled salsa
Topping: 1 avocado, peeled, pitted, and sliced; or 1 cup guacamole (page 50)

1. Heat oil in a skillet, add onion, and sauté for 2 minutes, stirring occasionally.

2. Add tofu cubes and sauté for 5 to 7 minutes, turning cubes occasionally, until tofu is slightly browned.

3. Add tortilla chips and stir to blend in with tofu. (You can break the chips up a little, if you want.) Cook for about 2 minutes, stirring occasionally.

4. Add salsa and cook for about 2 minutes, until tortillas start to soften and salsa is heated through. Serves 4.

Breakfast Brainstorm:
What Do YOU Eat in the A.M.?

"I buy a lot of dried fruits and nuts, and mix them with puffed grain cereal. I don't always have time to eat at home, so I put it in a bag and take it to school, along with some apple juice. I also bring granola bars to school."　　　　　　　　　**—Patrick, 16**

"I need a big breakfast, otherwise I feel really out of it by lunch. I buy enriched bagels and enriched cereal. If you are a vegan, a great way to get lots of vitamins like vitamin B_{12} is to have cereal that's fortified with them. I also try to have a different kind of fruit each day to keep things from getting boring."　　　　　　　　**—Erin, 16**

"Fresh fruit always rocks—apples, oranges, and bananas, especially."　　　　　　　　　　　　　　　　　　　　**—Maureen, 18**

"When I make pancakes or waffles, I top them with fresh fruit instead of syrup, and I always love to put peanut butter on them."　　　　　　　　　　　　　　　　　　　　**—Jason G., 19**

"A lot of kids don't realize how good plain old oatmeal is. It's great with fruit, maple syrup, whatever!"　　　　　　　**—Mollie, 19**

"Sometimes I eat pizza for breakfast. I also eat leftover Chinese food. Vegetable Lo Mein is really good cold. Breakfast doesn't have to be breakfast food!"　　　　　　　　　　　　**—Sheri, 15**

Tempeh Bacon

   3 Tablespoons barbecue sauce (mesquite or
      hickory smoke flavored is best)
   ⅓ cup water
   2 Tablespoons vegetable oil
   1½ teaspoons soy sauce
   1 Tablespoon liquid smoke flavoring,
      optional (available in supermarkets in
      the condiment section), or you could
      substitute a little extra barbecue sauce
      instead
   4 ounces tempeh, sliced into thin strips (see
      page 175)

1. To make marinade: In a shallow bowl, mix together all ingredients except for tempeh.

2. Add tempeh strips to marinade and let sit for at least 10 minutes.

3. Heat a nonstick skillet, remove tempeh from marinade (but save marinade), and place on pan. (You may have to do this in batches, depending on pan size.) Brown tempeh strips for a couple of minutes, turning occasionally, and add a couple tablespoons marinade to pan.

4. Continue cooking for about 5 minutes, turning occasionally and adding marinade when pan becomes dry. Strips are finished when they are just slightly blackened on each side. Remove and place on paper towel-lined plate to drain excess oil before serving. Makes about 4 servings.

Chunky Hash Browns

   3 medium potatoes, peeled and chopped into
      small pieces
   1 medium onion, finely chopped
   3 Tablespoons vegetable oil

2 cloves garlic, finely chopped
Salt and pepper to taste

1. Heat oil in skillet. Add onion and sauté for 2 or 3 minutes.
2. Add potatoes and stir to combine. Cook over medium heat for about 10 minutes, turning potatoes often. Stir in garlic. Cook potatoes for about 15 to 20 minutes in all, or until they are soft and golden brown. Serve with ketchup, salsa, or a sprinkling of soy or dairy cheese. Serves 2.

Why Do People Become Vegetarians?

*There are many reasons. Most of the teens I know who have become vegetarians have done it because they care about **animals**. "I didn't feel like it was right to kill animals to eat them," says Craig, 13. He and other teens oppose the cruel conditions in which farm animals are kept. (About 90 percent of the animals that people eat in the United States are raised in confinement.) For more information on this, read* Animal Factories *by Jim Mason and Peter Singer (Harmony Books). You can also contact People for the Ethical Treatment of Animals through its web site (www.peta-online.org) or at 501 Front Street, Norfolk, VA 23510.*

*Some teens go vegetarian because they care about the **environment**. Meat production uses vast amounts of land, grain, water, and energy resources and creates pollution. A vegetarian diet saves energy. A vegan diet is the most energy efficient. It takes more than three times as much fossil fuel energy to feed a meat eater as it does to feed a person who eats no meat or dairy products. For more information on how a vegetarian diet helps the planet, contact EarthSave International (www.earthsave.org), 600 Distillery Commons, Louisville, KY 40204-1922.*

*Other teens go vegetarian because they know how **healthy** a choice it is. Vegetarians have less heart disease and are less likely to get some types of cancer. And as a vegetarian, you can get all of the nutrients that your body needs. The American Dietetic Association has officially said that a vegetarian diet can be a nutritious way to eat, even for teens and children. For more information about nutrition, health, and other vegetarian issues, read* A Teen's Guide to Going Vegetarian *by Judy Krizmanic (Viking and Puffin Books).*

Variation: For **Hash Browns with Veggies,** add **1 cup chopped broccoli, mushrooms, and/or zucchini** toward end of cooking time; cover and cook a few more minutes until veggies are done.

Note: For faster-cooking hash browns, use **leftover baked potatoes** or cook potatoes first in the microwave oven. (Wash potatoes, pierce with fork, and bake for about 8 minutes on high.) Make sure cooked potato has cooled a bit before cutting it into small chunks. Reduce total cooking time to 5 to 10 minutes.

> ### What Kind of Vegetarian Are You?
>
> *There are all kinds of vegetarians:* **Lacto-ovo vegetarians** *eat no meat but do eat other animal products like eggs, milk, cheese, and honey.* **Lacto-vegetarians** *don't eat eggs but do use milk products. A person who follows a* **vegan** *(pronounced VEE-gun) diet eats no animal products at all. A vegan may also avoid using leather, wool, silk, and goose down.*

Vegan Banana Berry Muffins

A basic banana muffin gets a surprise of tangy berries. You can substitute other fruit for the berries, such as chopped peaches, apples, or dried apricots. For more tips on baking without eggs, see page 156.

2 cups unbleached white flour
1 teaspoon baking powder
1½ teaspoons baking soda
¼ teaspoon salt
1 cup mashed ripe banana (about 2
    medium bananas)
½ cup maple syrup, honey, or barley malt
6 Tablespoons vegetable oil
1 teaspoon vanilla extract
¼ teaspoon lemon extract
½ cup water
½ cup fresh or frozen blueberries,
    raspberries, or cranberries

1. Heat oven to 375° F. In a large bowl, combine flour, baking powder, baking soda, and salt.

2. In a medium-sized bowl, combine remaining ingredients, except berries. Pour this into flour mixture and stir until just combined. (Do not stir any longer, or muffins might be tough.)

3. Add berries and stir to distribute them throughout the batter. Spoon the batter into greased muffin tins to ⅔ full. (You can line the muffin tin with paper or foil liners instead of greasing).

4. Bake for about 20 minutes, or until muffins are risen, firm, and slightly golden on top. Makes about 8 to 10 muffins.

Hot Cereal Heaven

*Break your morning monotony by trying a new and unusual grain, such as **amaranth, couscous,** or **millet**. (See grain chart on page 115 for cooking times.) Also try **grits** and **cornmeal** (follow package directions). These hot cereals have a mild taste on their own, but you can jazz them up with your favorite fruits and spices. For instance, to make **Apricot Spice Hot Cereal,** add a small handful of **chopped dried apricots,** a few **raisins,** plus a dash of **cinnamon** and **ginger** to plain cooked cereal. Top with **soymilk** and maybe some **maple syrup**.*

LUNCHTIME

" *Was last night's dinner really good? Slap it between bread.* **"**

—Jason F.

What do you do when all your friends head to the cafeteria line for burgers and sausage pizza? You might find a few vegetarian things on your school's menu, but lots of vegetarian teens decide to take their lunches to school. But that doesn't mean you're doomed to peanut butter sandwiches forever.

Try these lunch ideas. Some can be thrown together right before school. Some you can make ahead of time. Planning ahead can help; if you make a batch of Chickpea Salad, No Egg Salad, or other sandwich fillings on the weekend, you're set for most of the week.

Sandwich Fillings

Pile these sandwich fillings on your favorite bread. Top them with tomatoes, lettuce, sprouts, whatever. If your sandwich is going to be sitting a long time in your backpack or locker, you might want to carry the filling in a separate plastic container and assemble the sandwich right before you eat it, to keep things from getting soggy.

insanely**easy**

Chickpea Salad

This recipe comes from vegetarian teen Jason F. It's kind of like a fake tuna salad. Good on bread or crackers, too. (Try it on seasoned matzo crackers.)

15 ounce can chickpeas, drained and rinsed
⅓ to ½ cup tofu mayonnaise (store-bought or homemade, page 28)
1½ stalks celery, cut into small pieces
½ teaspoon onion powder

½ teaspoon garlic powder
Salt and pepper to taste

1. In a bowl, mash chickpeas with a potato masher or fork. They don't have to be super-smooth; some chunks are fine.
2. Stir in remaining ingredients until well combined. Makes enough salad for about 4 sandwiches, and keeps in the refrigerator for several days.

insanely**easy**

No Egg Salad

8 ounces firm tofu, drained and crumbled
1 stalk celery, finely chopped
1 scallion, finely chopped
3 Tablespoons tofu mayonnaise
1 teaspoon Dijon mustard
Salt and pepper to taste

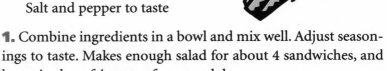

1. Combine ingredients in a bowl and mix well. Adjust seasonings to taste. Makes enough salad for about 4 sandwiches, and keeps in the refrigerator for several days.

Variation: Add your favorite **finely chopped veggies** to the salad, such as **carrots, bell peppers, zucchini,** or **yellow squash.**

insanely**easy**
Make Your Own Tofu Mayonnaise
Some of the recipes in this book call for tofu mayonnaise. Many vegetarians use tofu mayonnaise because it doesn't contain eggs. You can buy it in a natural foods store, or make it yourself. Here's how:

10 ounce package soft or silken tofu (about 1 cup)
1 Tablespoon plus 1 teaspoon vegetable oil
2 Tablespoons lemon juice
1½ to 2 teaspoons Dijon mustard
Dash of salt

Blend everything together in a food processor or blender until smooth. Use as you would use regular mayonnaise. Keeps in the refrigerator for several days.

insanely**easy**

Hummus

"I like hummus sandwiches in pita," says Erin, 16. "With pita bread, the filling doesn't squirt out on you when you eat it." Hummus sandwiches are good topped with grated carrots or sprouts.

> 15 ounce can chickpeas, drained and rinsed
> 3 to 4 Tablespoons tahini (sesame butter)
> 2 cloves garlic, peeled
> Juice of one lemon
> Salt and pepper to taste
> *Optional ingredients:*
> > 1 scallion, finely chopped (or 1 teaspoon onion powder)
> > 1 Tablespoon chopped fresh parsley
> > Dash of olive oil

> **No-Effort Nutrition Tip**
> *Choosing whole wheat bread (and pita pockets and tortillas) is an easy way to add extra nutrients to your sandwiches. Whole wheat breads have more B vitamins, vitamin E, and fiber than white breads.*

1. Blend all ingredients in a food processor or blender. Or mash everything in a bowl with a sturdy potato masher (if you use this method, finely chop or press the garlic first). Use as a sandwich spread or dip. Leftovers keep for about a week in the refrigerator.

Baba Ghanouj

This Middle Eastern dip (pronounced bah-bah guh-NOOSH) is kind of like hummus, but it's made with eggplant instead of chickpeas.

> 2 medium eggplants
> 4 Tablespoons tahini (sesame butter)
> 2 cloves garlic, finely chopped or pressed
> Juice of 1 lemon
> 2 Tablespoons chopped fresh parsley (optional)
> Salt and pepper to taste

1. Heat oven to 300° F. Pierce eggplants with a fork, place on a baking sheet, and bake until eggplants begin to wrinkle and deflate, at least 40 minutes. Let cool completely.

2. Slice eggplants in half, scoop insides into a bowl, and mash with a fork. Add remaining ingredients and mix well.

Variation: For **Spicy Baba Ghanouj,** add a **2 ounce jar pimientos,** well mashed, and **2 to 3 teaspoons hot sauce.** If a food processor or blender is available, blend the mixture until smooth.

Sun-dried Tomato Spread

My friend Jacqueline uses this on sandwiches and crackers, or even tossed with pasta.

¾ cup sun-dried tomatoes (the kind in a bag, not the kind bottled in oil)
Hot water
2 cloves garlic, peeled
8 to 10 fresh basil leaves
2 to 3 Tablespoons olive oil
Salt and pepper to taste

1. Place the tomatoes in a bowl, cover them with hot water, and let soak for about 15 minutes, or until soft. Drain the tomatoes and squeeze out excess water.

2. Place tomatoes and remaining ingredients in a blender or food processor and blend until the mixture is well combined. You can make it smooth or chunky. Makes about 1 cup of spread. You can store any unused spread in the refrigerator for several days.

Seasoned Tofu Slices

Broiled tofu is an amazing vegetarian sandwich filling. It's so easy. You can make a bunch of these and use them all week.

1. Set the oven to broiler setting. Meanwhile, drain and press water from a **16 ounce package extra-firm, water-packed tofu** (see page 176 for pressing instructions).

2. Slice the tofu into sandwich-sized rectangles, squares, or triangles.

3. Coat slices with your **favorite sauce or dressing:**

- ■ For **Barbecued Tofu:** Coat tofu slices with bottled **barbecue sauce**.
- ■ For **Italian Tofu:** Coat tofu slices with bottled **Italian dressing** and maybe a sprinkling of **dried basil** or **oregano**. (Note: An oil-based dressing works better than an oil-free variety, because the oil helps to brown the tofu.
- ■ For **Curried Tofu:** Coat tofu with bottled curry sauce. To make your own sauce, combine **3 Tablespoons vegetable oil** with **1½ teaspoons curry powder, 1½ teaspoons maple syrup** or other sweetener, and **1½ teaspoons tamari or soy sauce**.
- ■ For **Sesame Tofu:** Coat tofu with a combination of **1 Tablespoon vegetable oil**, **2 Tablespoons sesame oil**, and **2 teaspoons tamari or soy sauce**.
- ■ For **Szechwan or Teriyaki Tofu:** Coat tofu slices with bottled **Szechwan or teriyaki sauce**.

4. Place tofu on a small foil-lined pan under the broiler for about 4 or 5 minutes on each side, turning occasionally during broiling. Broil until the tofu edges are browned and the tofu firms up a bit. Serve on sandwiches. Makes 6 to 8 slices.

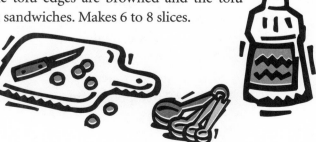

Eggplant Rounds

Cook up some of these eggplant rounds and you're ready to roll. Good with hummus in a sandwich, or with any of your favorite sandwich toppings.

> 1 medium eggplant
> 1 cup bottled Italian dressing (or other
>   non-creamy dressing)
> 1½ cup packaged bread crumbs
> Dash of salt

1. Set oven to broiler setting. Wash the eggplant and slice into ½-inch thick rounds.

2. Pour dressing into a bowl and pour bread crumbs onto a plate. Dip each eggplant slice into the dressing and then coat with bread crumbs.

3. Place a few coated eggplant rounds on a piece of foil and place under the broiler for about 4 or 5 minutes on each side, or until lightly browned.

4. Remove from broiler and use a spatula to lift the eggplant round onto your sandwich. Repeat with remaining eggplant rounds. Store cooked eggplant rounds in the refrigerator. You can eat them cold, or reheated in a microwave or toaster oven.

Note: Instead of broiling, you can pan-fry the rounds in a little vegetable oil or olive oil, turning occasionally, until lightly browned on each side (about 8 minutes total).

Sesame Tofu Triangles

Sweet, spicy, and unique! Try these triangles in a pita or rolled up into a whole wheat tortilla, or even without bread.

> 16 ounce package extra-firm, water-packed
>   tofu
> 1 Tablespoon vegetable oil
> 2 Tablespoons sesame oil
> 4 Tablespoons water
> 1½ to 2 Tablespoons tamari or soy sauce

2 teaspoons apple cider vinegar or rice
   vinegar
1 Tablespoon barley malt or honey
⅛ teaspoon cayenne pepper
1 scallion, chopped
2 Tablespoons red bell pepper, finely chopped
Dash of garlic powder (optional)
Dash of ground ginger (optional)
Sesame seeds for sprinkling

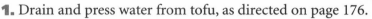

1. Drain and press water from tofu, as directed on page 176.
2. In a large sealable container, combine remaining ingredients, except sesame seeds.
3. When tofu is drained, cut it into ½ inch slices; then cut slices diagonally to form triangles. You can make the triangles as big or as small as you'd like. Place tofu triangles into marinade, seal container, and turn container over a few times to coat the pieces well. Let sit for about 10 minutes.
4. To cook, heat a large skillet over medium heat. Lift tofu triangles into the pan with a spatula, and pour half of the marinade into the pan. Sauté the tofu, turning occasionally, until firm and slightly browned on both sides. Add a little more marinade if liquid begins to cook away.
5. When the tofu is finished cooking, place in bowl with remaining marinade, and sprinkle with sesame seeds. Cover and store in the refrigerator until chilled. Makes about 4 servings.

The Lucky Lunch Box

Try some of these ideas to round out your lunch:

Fresh fruit
Fresh veggies, such as carrots, green
   peppers, celery, lettuce, mushrooms,
   and cherry tomatoes
Crackers and rice cakes
Mixtures of dried fruits or nuts
Popcorn
Small cans of applesauce or fruit
Fruit leathers
Small boxes of soymilk
A homemade snack. "For a real treat,
   make some eggless cookies with nuts
   and fruit and pack 'em for lunch,"
   says Maureen, 18.

Sandwich Station

Got the PB&J blues? Pick your favorite things from
each column to design your own ultimate sandwich. Add any
other toppings you can think of, too.

Bread	Spread	Filling	Topping
Select 1 from this column	*Select 1*	*Select 1 or 2*	*Select 1 or 2 or more*
Whole wheat bread slices Enriched white bread slices Bagel, sliced Pita pocket Large tortilla Dark brown bread slices (like rye or pumpernickel) Submarine sandwich roll	Mustard (Dijon is good) Ketchup Tofu mayonnaise (store bought or homemade, page 28) Sun-dried Tomato Spread, page 30 Favorite creamy salad dressing Mixture of tahini (sesame butter) and yogurt	Vegetarian lunch meat slices* Hummus (page 29) Baba Ghanouj (page 29) Falafel balls (Middle Eastern chickpea patties) made from a box mix Avocado slices Soy or dairy cheese slices Veggie burger (precooked) Seasoned Tofu Slices (page 31) Basic Bean Dip (page 51) Curried or bar-becued tempeh patties (pages 35–36) Bean There, Done That Salsa (page 48) Eggplant Rounds (page 32) Sesame Tofu Triangles (page 32)	Grated carrots Lettuce leaves, shredded lettuce, or sprouts Grated beets Zucchini slices Cucumber slices Sliced tomatoes Finely sliced red onion Chopped broccoli Chopped cauliflower Grated green or red cabbage Grated soy or dairy cheese

*Vegetarian lunch meat slices come in many varieties at the natural foods store: bologna, turkey, chicken, pastrami, pepperoni, Canadian bacon, and others.

Curried Tempeh Sandwiches

Tempeh is a soyfood that is great for sandwiches because it comes in a convenient patty shape. Slice it, season it, and cook it.

3 Tablespoons vegetable oil
¾ cup water
1 Tablespoon tamari or soy sauce
1 to 2 teaspoons curry powder (depending on how hot you'd like it)
2 teaspoons apple juice concentrate, honey, or sugar
1 Tablespoon apple cider vinegar
8 ounce package tempeh

1. To make sauce: Combine all ingredients except for tempeh in a bowl or shallow baking dish.

2. Slice tempeh into 6 to 8 sandwich-sized patties. Put in sauce, making sure to coat all slices, and let sit at least 10 minutes.

3. Heat a nonstick skillet or sauté pan, and lift the tempeh slices from curry sauce (but save sauce) and place them in the pan. Sauté for about 3 or 4 minutes over medium heat, turning occasionally, until tempeh slices start to brown slightly.

4. Reduce heat to low and pour the curry sauce over the tempeh. Cover and cook for about 5 minutes, turning occasionally, until sauce has almost disappeared and tempeh is browned.

5. Remove from heat and serve on bread with your favorite sandwich toppings (tomato, lettuce, and cucumber are good). Makes 3 or 4 sandwiches.

Lunchtime Survival Tips

"If you're nervous about your new diet, I wouldn't take too many strange-looking things to school until you're comfortable with it," says Erin, 16. You might start out with familiar things like peanut butter and jelly, and then slowly add some more unusual foods. "And I wouldn't recommend trying new foods for the first time in front of everyone at the lunch table. If you're always saying how good vegetarian food is, and you don't like it, you can end up looking pretty silly."

Zesty BBQ Burgers

½ cup bottled barbecue sauce
½ cup water
2 Tablespoons vegetable oil
8 ounce package tempeh

1. Combine barbecue sauce, water, and oil in a bowl. Set aside.
2. Slice tempeh into 6 to 8 sandwich-sized patties. Place tempeh patties in barbecue sauce mixture and let sit for at least 10 minutes.
3. Heat a nonstick skillet or sauté pan, and lift the tempeh slices from sauce (but save sauce) and place them in the pan. Sauté for about 3 or 4 minutes over medium heat, turning occasionally, until tempeh slices start to brown slightly.
4. Reduce heat to low and pour the sauce over the tempeh. Cover and cook for about 5 minutes, turning occasionally, until sauce has almost disappeared and tempeh starts to darken.
5. Remove from heat and serve on bread with your favorite sandwich toppings (tomato, lettuce, and cucumber are good). Makes 3 or 4 sandwiches.

Lunch on the Run

❝This year, I have so many electives in my class schedule that I don't have time for a full lunch. I bring a lot of things that I can nibble on all day long: peanut butter and celery, cut up vegetables, grapes, leftover fruit salad, some type of bread. Yogurt is easy, too. Sometimes I'll have pita and cream cheese. I try to bring some things that don't make a lot of noise in class. I'm also really big on leftovers. Pizza is really easy; just wrap it in tin foil. If we eat out on Saturday night, I can bring that to school for a few days. By the time I get sick of that, there's usually some new leftover.❞

—**Sheri, 15**

Cold Sesame Noodles

*This tasty dish is easy to transport. Make some at night to take to
school the next day.*

8 ounces rotini or other pasta (Japanese soba
noodles are good, too)

4 Tablespoons tahini
(sesame butter)

2 teaspoons sesame oil

2 teaspoons tamari or soy
sauce

2 cloves garlic, peeled and
very finely chopped

½ teaspoon finely
chopped fresh ginger root
(peeled first) or ¼ teaspoon dried ginger

1½ teaspoons barley malt, honey, or frozen
apple juice concentrate

1 teaspoon rice vinegar

3 Tablespoons water

1 Tablespoon lemon juice

1 scallion, finely chopped

¼ cup frozen green peas, thawed (or use
trimmed and sliced snow peas)

¼ cup very thin sliced carrot strips, about
1½ inch long (you can start with the
prepackaged baby carrots)

> **"***For those delicious tomato-and-
> mozzarella-on-Italian-bread sandwiches
> that I used to love, I replace the moz-
> zarella with slices of tofu soaked in a
> combination of olive oil and salt and
> garlic powder.***"**   **—Tovah, 16**

1. Cook the pasta according to
package directions or directions on
page 90.

2. While pasta is cooking, combine
tahini, sesame oil, tamari or soy
sauce, garlic, ginger, barley malt or
other sweetener, rice vinegar, water,
and lemon juice to make the sauce.

3. When pasta is done cooking,

> ### Fresh and Fruity Idea
> *Use fresh fruit on your sandwich.
> Top peanut butter with banana
> slices, peaches, or fresh berries
> instead of jelly. Add fresh apple
> slices to a plain cheese sandwich.*

drain noodles and toss with the sauce. Add onions, peas, and carrots and mix together (you can save some vegetables to use as a garnish, if you want). Adjust sauce seasonings to suit your taste. Chill for 2 hours before serving. Serves 2 to 4.

insanelyeasy

Gingery Carrot Raisin Salad
This sweet little side-salad will cheer up any lunch. Pack in a sealable container.

2½ cups shredded carrots (you can use
    a hand grater or food processor)
⅓ cup raisins
1½ Tablespoons lemon juice
1½ Tablespoons brown sugar, maple
    syrup, barley malt, or orange juice
    concentrate
⅛ teaspoon ground ginger

1. Combine carrots and raisins in a medium-sized bowl.

2. In a separate bowl, combine remaining ingredients and stir well. Pour over carrot-raisin mixture and stir to combine. Serves 4.

Variation: For a more filling salad, add **1 cup cooked or canned chickpeas,** drained and rinsed.

> **A Nutty Idea**
> *For variety, use a different nut butter instead of peanut butter on your sandwiches, such as cashew butter, almond butter, or hazelnut butter. You can find these in natural foods stores and some supermarkets.*

More Portable Lunches

Anything in a Thermos: "I make soup or potatoes and keep them in a thermos, and take crackers or bread along with them," says Johanna, 19. A wide-mouth thermos is really handy. You can pack chili, noodles, mashed potatoes and veggie gravy, refried beans, cooked vegetables, even pancake or waffle pieces with syrup.

Recycled Sandwich: "Was last night's dinner really good? Slap it between bread," suggests Jason F. "All of those grain and bean loaves work well for this. Also, you can cook the water out of a bean dish, refrigerate, and the next morning . . . voilà! Spread it on."

> ### Pack a Pita! Roll a Tortilla!
> ■ *Don't overstuff pita bread, or it will break apart.*
> ■ *If your pita seems dry, you can sprinkle a little water on it, wrap it in aluminum foil, and heat it briefly in the oven or a toaster oven.*
> ■ *To prevent soggy pitas, carry your filling in a separate container and fill the pita just before eating.*
> ■ *Tortilla wrapped sandwiches travel best when tightly secured in plastic wrap or foil.*

Packaged Veggie Burgers, Veggie Dogs: Cook the burgers or dogs quickly before school, put them on a bun, and add favorite toppings.

Baked Potato: Wrap a baked potato in foil and pack in an insulated lunch bag to hold in the heat. Or cut the potato in half and place in a wide-mouth thermos. You can top your potato with salsa, canned vegetarian chili, or an instant bean-and-rice cup meal, available at natural food stores or supermarkets.

Pasta Salad: See recipes, pages 109–11. Or, thaw **2 cups store-bought frozen pasta and vegetable mixture** (available in bags at any supermarket), add your favorite **salad dressing** and a sprinkling of **soy or dairy cheese**.

Frozen Yogurt: Freeze yogurt overnight, wrap in a small towel (to

> *"It's amazing how much becoming a vegan has changed my perspective. I see a lot more injustices than I used to. I'm also aware of solutions and positive things we can do with our food and product choices to better the world, or at least refrain from harming it."*
>
> **—Josh, 17, who became a vegan at age 15**

absorb the moisture), and pack it in your lunch bag. The yogurt will still be cold at lunch time. You may want to try soy yogurt or organic dairy yogurt, available at natural foods stores.

VBLT Sandwich: The V is for vegetarian: Use store-bought or homemade tempeh bacon (page 21), lettuce, and tomato on bread. For an interesting variation, try spreading the bread with peanut butter first.

Instant Soups or Meals-in-a-Cup: All you have to do is add hot water, which you can get almost anywhere.

Peanut Butter Pancake Sandwiches: Use leftover pancakes or waffles, spread with peanut butter. Add some fresh fruit or shredded carrots, if you want.

"Just the other day I had to answer my friend's questions about being a vegetarian. I'm happy because I think she gets it. Maybe she'll decide to go veggie. If she does, I'll be thrilled, but if she doesn't it's okay. Friendships are about respecting each other." **—Andrea, 19**

SNACKS AND DIPS

"My favorite snack is trail mix. I put lots of different stuff in it— anything I find appealing."

—Amy, 16

Just about anything can be a snack. Next time you're starving after school or looking for munchies for your friends, try some of these.

Nacho Cheeseless Sauce

You'd swear this stuff was made from cheese. Serve with tortilla chips.

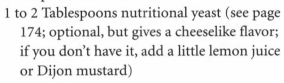

12 ounce package soft or silken tofu
½ cup bottled salsa
¼ teaspoon salt, or to taste
¼ teaspoon turmeric
1 to 2 Tablespoons nutritional yeast (see page 174; optional, but gives a cheeselike flavor; if you don't have it, add a little lemon juice or Dijon mustard)
¼ cup water mixed with 1 Tablespoon corn-starch
1 Tablespoon vegetable oil

1. In a blender, puree tofu, salsa, salt, turmeric, and water-cornstarch mixture (and nutritional yeast, if using).
2. Heat oil in a skillet and make sure bottom of pan is coated. Pour in tofu mixture and spread to cover pan. Cook tofu mixture on low heat for about 5 minutes, without stirring.
3. Use a wooden spoon or spatula to mix up the tofu, stirring to get a creamy consistency. Pour/scrape sauce into a bowl and serve with chips. Serves 4 to 6.

Variation: For a spicier sauce, add **2 Tablespoons chopped canned green chilies** to tofu mixture before cooking.

To make **Loaded Nachos:** Spread some **canned black, pinto, or vegetarian refried beans** onto a plate. (If using black or pinto beans, drain first.) Warm in a microwave. Top with **salsa,** warm **Nacho Cheeseless Sauce, shredded lettuce,** and **chopped tomato.** Serve with **tortilla chips.**

insanely**easy**

Pita Pizzas

> 2 pieces of pita bread (or French bread,
>   English muffins, or bagels)
> ½ cup bottled spaghetti sauce
> A few chopped veggies, such as broccoli,
>   green pepper, mushroom, tomato
> ½ cup grated soy cheese or dairy cheese
>   (optional)

1. Heat oven or toaster oven to 350° F. Spread bread with spaghetti sauce and top with veggies and cheese, if using. If omitting cheese, top veggies with a little sauce to keep them from drying out.

2. Place in the oven or toaster oven and bake for 6 to 8 minutes. Serves 1 or 2.

> ❝A snack I like is Ants on a Log. You take celery sticks and put peanut butter in the hollowed-out part, then put raisins on top of the peanut butter. The raisins are supposed to be the ants.❞ **—Kathleen, 17**

Squashadillas

You're probably familiar with quesadillas made from tortillas and cheese. Squashadillas look deceptively similar—but they're dairy free. Cut them into triangles and dip in salsa for a great party snack.

> 2 to 2½ cups leftover cooked butternut
>   squash (page 137 or 140) or frozen squash
>   warmed in the microwave
> ⅔ cup bottled salsa
> Pinch of salt (optional)
> 8 small flour tortillas
> Toppings: salsa, tomatoes, tofu sour cream
>   (page 51), or guacamole (page 50)

1. Combine squash, salsa, and salt, if using, in a bowl.

2. Spread ¼ of mixture onto one tortilla and top with another tortilla. Press down lightly to make sure tortillas hold together while cooking. (You can also make half-sized squashadillas by spreading filling over ½ of a tortilla and folding it over.)

3. Heat a nonstick griddle or large nonstick frying pan and place the squashadilla on the griddle. Heat for about 2 minutes, use a spatula to flip squashadilla, and heat for 2 minutes more. Continue flipping and heating until golden brown and starting to crisp on both sides, about 5 or 6 minutes in all. Use spatula to transfer to a plate, cool for a minute, and cut into halves, quarters, or wedges. Repeat for each squashadilla.

Variation: For **Beanadillas,** substitute a **15 ounce can vegetarian refried beans** for the squash. Add **soy or dairy cheese** if desired.

> ### insanely**easy**
> ### Sheri's Healthy Banana Split
> ❝*Take a **banana** and slice it down the middle the long way. Then take some all-natural **chunky peanut butter** and spread it on the inside of each banana half. Put the slice back together so you have a banana-peanut butter sandwich. Then cut the banana into slices so that they form circular sandwiches. I pick up the little sandwiches with a fork and pop them into my mouth.*❞   **—Sheri, 15**

insanely**easy**

Peanut Butter Balls

Carol Coughlin, a registered dietitian, makes these snacks for her family. They're inexpensive, fun to make, and a good alternative to candy bars.

¼ cup low fat granola
2 Tablespoons brown sugar
¼ cup raisins
¼ cup finely shredded carrots
¾ cup peanut butter

1. Combine all ingredients except peanut butter in a bowl. Set aside.

2. Heat peanut butter in the microwave for 45 seconds to soften, or heat in a small saucepan on the stovetop.

3. Add peanut butter to granola mixture and stir to combine.

> Remember: Many of the sandwich fill-
> ings in the Lunch section—such as
> Chickpea Salad, Hummus, and Baba
> Ghanouj—make delicious snacks, too.
> Serve them as dips with crackers, chips,
> or pita triangles.

4. Let the mixture cool, and roll into small balls. Makes about 12 balls.

Potato Puffs

These puffs make great party snacks. Use your imagination to fill puffs with whatever you'd like—leftover vegetables, chili and cheese—you name it.

1 tube refrigerated crescent roll dough (read
    label and make sure it's lard-free)
1½ cups or so leftover mashed potatoes or
    leftover Potatoes and Greens (page 142)
¼ to ½ cup grated soy or dairy parmesan
    cheese (optional)

> **"**I like to spread rice cakes with peanut
> butter and then top them with cut-up vege-
> tables, like carrots and celery. Arrange the
> vegetables into faces. It's a snack that's full
> of creativity and protein.**"**   **—Sheri, 15**

1. Heat oven to 375° F. Separate the dough into triangles and place on an ungreased baking sheet.
2. Place a scoop of potato filling, and a sprinkling of cheese if using, near the center of each triangle and wrap triangle points around the filling in a freeform manner to make little bundles, leaving some potato mixture showing in the middle. (To prevent sticking, make sure the base of the bundle is completely made of dough so that no potato mixture contacts the baking sheet.)
3. Bake for about 15 to 17 minutes, or until pastry is puffed and golden brown. Makes 8.

insanelyeasy

Tofu Dogs in a Blanket

8 tofu hot dogs (available at natural foods
    stores)

1 tube refrigerated crescent roll dough (read
   label and make sure it's lard free)

1. Remove soy hot dogs from their package. Open and separate
the dough into triangles and place on an ungreased baking
sheet. Roll one soy dog into each triangle.

2. Bake for about 15 minutes, or until dough is golden brown.
Remove from oven, cool briefly, and slice the baked tofu dogs
into halves. Share with friends. Makes 16 pieces. (To serve for
lunch, leave the baked dogs whole.)

   Variation: Before rolling up the dog, spread the dough with
Dijon mustard, tofu mayonnaise, or **salsa,** or sprinkle dough
with **grated soy or dairy cheese.**

Some Quick and Easy Snacks

- *Leftover pizza*
- *Fruit salad*
- *Cut-up celery sticks, carrots, broccoli, or cauliflower
  (keep them on hand in the fridge and eat plain
  or with dip)*
- *Rice cakes with hummus (page 29)*
- *Pretzels and dip*
- *Popcorn seasoned with curry powder or vegetable
  seasoning blend*
- *Cookies and soymilk*
- *Muffins (page 23)*
- *A bowl of leftover soup*
- *Sweet potato un-fries (page 143)*
- *Chips and salsa (pages 48–50)*
- *Instant soup cups or bean-and-rice cups*
- *A handful of raisins or dried apricots*
- *Bagels with peanut butter*
- *Bagels or rice cakes with tofu mayonnaise
  (page 28), avocado, and tomato slices*
- *Cornbread slices (page 147) with avocado
  and salsa*
- *Soy or dairy yogurt*
- *Hot chocolate made with soymilk or rice milk*

Tamari Nuts

These seasoned nuts have a sweet and salty kick to them. Good for get-togethers.

    1 cup walnuts, cashews, almonds,
        peanuts, or sunflower seeds (or a
        combination)
    1 to 1½ Tablespoons tamari or soy
        sauce

> **"***My favorite snack is trail mix. I put lots of different stuff in it: cereal, nuts, seeds, and anything else I find appealing.***"**
>   **—Amy, 16**

1. Heat oven to 350° F. Spread nuts on a baking sheet and toast them by baking for about 15 to 20 minutes, stirring once during baking. Remove nuts from oven and slide them from the pan into a bowl.
2. Drizzle on tamari or soy sauce, toss or stir to coat, and place nuts back on the baking sheet. Bake for a few more minutes, remove from oven, and let cool. Serves 4.

Salsas and Dips

The following recipes make great chip dips and cracker spreads, but you can also use some of them in sandwiches or in burritos.

Bean There, Done That Salsa

My friend David made up this easy salsa recipe. For a variation, add a chopped avocado. Serve with tortilla chips or potato chips or as a pita sandwich filling.

    15 ounce can black beans, drained and
        rinsed
    1 to 1½ cups frozen vegetable medley (a
        blend of corn, peppers, and green beans
        works well; plain corn is good, too)
    1 cup salsa

¼ cup chopped fresh cilantro
Splash of lime or lemon juice
Salt and pepper to taste

1. In a large bowl, combine all ingredients. Let salsa sit until frozen veggies are thawed. Stir. Serves 4 to 6.

Simple Sunflower Seed Salsa

Fresh salsa is so much tastier than the bottled kind. This one includes sunflower seeds for an unusual crunch. Serve with tortilla chips.

2 medium tomatoes, chopped
A big handful of cilantro, chopped
½ medium-sized onion, chopped
2 Tablespoons shelled sunflower seeds
Juice of ½ lime (1–2 teaspoons)
½ teaspoon salt
½ teaspoon pepper
¼ to ½ teaspoon crushed red chili
    flakes (optional)
¼ teaspoon dried cumin

1. Combine all ingredients in a bowl. Let salsa sit a little while to give flavors a chance to blend. Serves 4 to 6.

Gwenn's Mango Salsa

Who says salsa must be made of tomatoes? Serve with tortilla or toasted pita chips, or as a topping over sautéed tofu or tempeh patties.

2 ripe mangoes, peeled, pitted, and diced
⅓ red onion, diced
Juice from ½ lime
¼ cup fresh cilantro, chopped
½ fresh jalapeño pepper, seeded and diced
    (see *Jalapeño Pepper Pointers*, page 50)

Pinch of salt
Dash of olive oil or vegetable oil
½ teaspoon sugar or frozen apple juice
concentrate (optional)

1. Combine all ingredients in a large bowl. Let salsa sit a little while before serving to give flavors a chance to blend. Serves 4 to 6.

Jalapeño Pepper Pointers

Jalapeño peppers are small (about 3 inches long) chili peppers that are bright green when fresh and red when dried. Jalapeños are pretty spicy, so you might want to use only a small amount in a recipe the first time you cook with them. To use: wash pepper, cut it open, and carefully remove and discard the seeds (the spiciest part). Chop the fleshy part of the pepper into small pieces. Wash your cutting board, knife, and hands after cutting jalapeño peppers and other hot chilies, and be careful not to rub your eyes—the natural pepper juice can really burn.

---

insanely**easy**

Great Guacamole

Good as a chip dip or on pita sandwiches or tacos. You can add hot sauce, cumin, or chili powder to season, if you'd like.

2 ripe avocados, peeled and pitted
2 Tablespoons finely chopped scallions or
regular onion
1 small tomato, finely chopped (optional)
Juice from ½ lemon (1–2 teaspoons, or more,
to taste)
Salt and pepper to taste

1. Combine all ingredients in a bowl. Adjust seasonings to taste, and serve. Serves 4 to 6.

Variation: Jessica, 15, suggests **Creamy Tofu Guacamole.** Just add to the above recipe: **12 ounce package silken tofu,** drained and mashed, a little **fresh chopped cilantro, garlic powder,** and maybe some **canned diced green chilies** or **hot sauce.**

insanely**easy**

Creamy Onion Dip

Serve with chips or cut-up fresh vegetables.

1 batch tofu sour cream
1 package instant onion
   soup mix

insanely**easy**

Homemade Tofu Sour Cream
*In a blender, combine a **12 ounce package silken tofu** (about 1 cup) with **1 Tablespoon plus 1 teaspoon vegetable oil, 2 Tablespoons lemon juice**, and a good **dash of salt**. Use this just like you would regular sour cream in recipes, dips, or as a topping for Mexican food.*

1. Combine ingredients in a bowl. Let dip chill in refrigerator for about an hour, or until flavors are blended and any onion pieces in the soup mix are soft.

Variation: For **Onion-Spinach Dip,** add ½ **to 1 10 ounce package frozen spinach** (thaw and press water out first).

insanely**easy**

Basic Bean Dip

15 ounce can black, pinto, or white
   beans, drained
⅔ cup salsa
Dash of cumin

1. Combine ingredients in a food processor (or use a potato masher to mash and combine in a bowl). Scoop into a bowl and serve with tortilla chips. Serves 4 to 6.

Variation: For **Cilantro White Bean Dip,** use **white beans,** skip the salsa, and add a little fresh chopped **cilantro** and a squirt of **lemon juice.**

For an **Instant Burrito,** heat the bean dip, spread on a tortilla, and roll up.

insanely**easy**

Tangy Thai Peanut Dip

Serve this dip with cut up veggies.

1 cup chunky natural peanut butter
¼ cup warm water

3 green onions, chopped
1 teaspoon fresh chopped ginger
¼ to ½ teaspoons cayenne pepper
2 Tablespoons tamari or soy sauce
3 Tablespoons lemon juice or rice vinegar
1 to 2 teaspoons apple juice concentrate,
    barley malt, or honey

1. Combine ingredients in a food processor or blender until smooth. To make a thinner dip, add a little extra warm water. Serves 6.

Variations: Add **2 Tablespoons chopped cilantro leaves** or ¼ **jalapeño chili pepper,** seeded and chopped (page 50).

Elegant Appetizers

Looking for something more sophisticated for a special gathering or event? These snacks are a little fancier, but still fuss-free.

Bruschetta: *Cut a long, slender loaf of* **crusty bread** *into thin slices. In small batches, place slices on a small cookie sheet or piece of foil, brush each side with* **olive oil,** *and broil for about 5 minutes on each side, or until lightly toasted. Meanwhile, mix together a couple of* **finely chopped tomatoes,** *a small handful of* **finely chopped fresh basil,** *a couple of* **finely chopped garlic cloves,** *a little* **olive oil** *and* **balsamic vinegar,** *and* **salt and pepper.** *When bread slices are toasted, top with tomato mixture and serve on a nice platter. (Top slices about an hour ahead to give juice a chance to soak into bread.)*

Pesto Polenta Wheels: *Start with a tube of* **pre-seasoned polenta,** *available in most supermarkets (try sun-dried tomato or mushroom flavor). Slice into rounds about ¼ inch thick, brush both sides thoroughly with* **olive oil,** *place on a cookie sheet, and bake at 375° F for about 20 minutes on each side, or until polenta pieces are golden. Top baked polenta rounds with a little* **bottled pesto** *and* **chopped tomato.** *You can also sprinkle with* **grated soy or dairy cheese.**

MAIN DISHES

"Don't be afraid of foods that sound like plastic tubing. TVP® is good stuff.**"**
                                    —Scott, 17

When the rest of your family sits down to dinner, you don't have to settle for their side dishes. "I always make my own dinners, usually entirely different from what the family is eating," says Mara, 17. "Even my meat-eating family enjoys many of the things I make."

If the thought of making an entire meal sounds scary, don't worry. You don't have to be a gourmet chef to whip up dinners that are easy and delicious. Experiment with the following dinner ideas, and don't forget to check out the pasta section (pages 89–102).

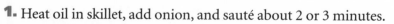

Sloppy Joes

Most supermarkets sell frozen veggie-burger crumbles, which you can use just like ground beef in a recipe. Grated tempeh makes a good hamburger substitute, too. If you like your Sloppy Joes even sloppier, add a little more tomato sauce.

    2 Tablespoons olive oil
    1 medium onion, finely chopped
    1½ to 2 cups store-bought frozen veggie-
        burger crumbles or grated tempeh (use
        a hand grater or food processor)
    1 Tablespoon tamari or soy sauce
    ½ green bell pepper, finely chopped
    8 ounce can tomato sauce
    1 teaspoon Dijon mustard
    2 Tablespoons ketchup
    ½ teaspoon chili powder
    1 to 2 teaspoons molasses or other sweetener
    4 burger buns or pita bread

1. Heat oil in skillet, add onion, and sauté about 2 or 3 minutes.

> **"**What would I tell a new vegetarian? For one thing, don't eat just vegetables. It's really dumb that people think that all vegetarians eat are vegetables. They don't think about other things, like noodles and rice. You should try TVP®, seitan, and I guess tofu, too, even though I personally don't like it, although I know some people who love it.**"** —**Sara, 15**

2. Add burger crumbles or tempeh and sauté another 3 minutes, until lightly browned. Add a little water if things look dry.

3. Add tamari or soy sauce and green pepper, combine, and sauté another minute or so. Add remaining ingredients (except for the bread) and stir. Cook for about 4 minutes or so, until heated through and flavors are combined.

4. Serve Sloppy Joe mixture on buns or in pita pockets. Makes about 4 sandwiches.

Create-Your-Own Veggie Burger Recipe

This recipe uses textured vegetable protein, or TVP®, which you can find in a natural foods store. "Don't be afraid of foods that sound like plastic tubing," says Scott, 17—TVP® is good stuff. Once you create the basic burger mix, you can season it any way you want. Suggestions are given below.

> 2 cups dried textured vegetable protein
>   granules (not the chunky kind)
> 1¾ cups boiling water
> 1 small onion, finely chopped
> ¾ teaspoon finely chopped fresh garlic or
>   garlic powder
> ½ teaspoon black pepper
> ¾ teaspoon salt
> 1 Tablespoon tamari or soy sauce
> 2 Tablespoons ketchup
> ¼ teaspoon chili powder
> ½ teaspoon cumin
> ¾ teaspoon oregano
> 1½ Tablespoons dried parsley

½ cup flour

2 to 3 Tablespoons vegetable or olive oil

1. Place textured vegetable protein in a bowl, add water, and let soak for 10 minutes.

2. Add onion, garlic, and all seasonings to textured vegetable protein and mix together. Add flour and mix well. Shape into burgers.

3. Heat oil in a skillet until very hot, and pan-fry burgers until golden brown on each side, about 10 minutes total.

Burger Variations:

For **Teriyaki Burgers,** substitute **2 Tablespoons teriyaki sauce** for the ketchup.

For **Sunflower Burgers,** add **¼ cup sunflower seeds.**

For **Sesame Burgers,** add **2 teaspoons dark sesame oil** and **3 Tablespoons sesame seeds.**

For **Dijon Burgers,** add **1 or 2 Tablespoons Dijon mustard.**

For **Salsa Burgers,** substitute **salsa** for ketchup and add **1 to 2 teaspoons hot sauce.**

For **Veggie Meatballs,** shape the mixture into balls instead of patties and cook as directed above.

Savory Roasted Seitan

16 ounce package seitan pieces (chicken-style works best)

4 to 6 cloves garlic, peeled and cut in half lengthwise

3 Tablespoons olive oil

1 Tablespoon dried parsley

1 teaspoon dried sage or poultry seasoning (see note)

Salt and pepper

1. Heat oven to 350°F. Cut seitan into bite-sized pieces and place in a small roasting pan. Add garlic, olive oil, parsley, sage or seasoning, and a generous sprinkling of salt and pepper. Cover with foil or lid and bake for 25 to 30 minutes, stirring once halfway through.

2. When the seitan is finished, remove from oven and serve with Easy Veggie Gravy.

Variation: Halfway through the baking, add **3 cups** washed, finely chopped **spinach** leaves, **Swiss chard** leaves or **other greens,** plus ⅔ **cup grated soy or dairy parmesan or cheddar cheese.** Stir to combine, replace lid and continue baking.

Note: Poultry seasoning doesn't contain any poultry; it's a mix of different herbs that are often used to season poultry dishes. It's available in any supermarket.

Easy Veggie Gravy

*In a large, deep skillet over medium heat, heat **4 Tablespoons oil** (half olive oil, half vegetable oil is good) for one minute. Add **6 Tablespoons flour** and stir together until pasty. Slowly add **3½ cups vegetable broth** (or part vegetable broth, part water), and stir with a whisk until smooth. Add **1 teaspoon poultry seasoning, ½ teaspoon apple cider vinegar, 1 teaspoon Dijon mustard,** and a **pinch of pepper.** Continue whisking. If the gravy seems too thick, add a little water. Adjust seasonings to taste. Makes about 4 cups.*

---

insanely**easy**

Tofu Italiano

Here's a recipe from my friends Karin and Matt. It's a fast-dinner favorite at their house. Serve this over cooked couscous or pasta.

2 Tablespoons olive oil
16 ounce package firm or extra-firm tofu,
    drained and cubed
2 cups store-bought pasta sauce
15 ounce can chickpeas, drained
¾ cup frozen corn kernels
¾ cup frozen green peas

1. Heat oil in a large saucepan or skillet. Add tofu cubes and cook for about 5 minutes, turning tofu frequently, until lightly browned on all sides.

2. Add remaining ingredients and cook for about 10 minutes over medium-low heat until chickpeas and vegetables are heated through. Serve over couscous or pasta. Serves 4.

Simple Veggie Sauté

Try this dish in the summer with fresh vegetables from the garden or farmers market.

> 1 cup brown rice or 8 ounces pasta
> 15 ounce can chickpeas, with liquid
> 2 cloves garlic, peeled and chopped
> 1 medium zucchini or yellow squash (or use
>   half of each)
> 1 small to medium green bell pepper, with
>   seeds removed, chopped
> Dash of salt
> 1 medium tomato, chopped
> ½ cup corn kernels (fresh off cob
>   or frozen)
> Sprinkling of fresh chopped basil or dried
>   basil
> Dash of pepper

1. Cook brown rice or noodles according to package directions (or see grain cooking instructions, page 115).

2. While rice or pasta is cooking, open can of chickpeas. Drain the liquid into a large skillet or saucepan and add garlic to the liquid. Set can of chickpeas aside. Simmer garlic in chickpea liquid for about 2 to 3 minutes over medium heat.

3. Add chopped zucchini or yellow squash, green pepper, and chickpeas and sprinkle with salt. Sauté for about 5 minutes.

4. Add chopped tomato, corn, and basil and cook for about 5 more minutes.

>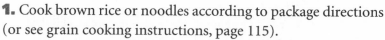
> **"** *Just don't give up if a new recipe doesn't turn out like you had hoped. Try it again, and if you still don't like it, don't worry about it. There are tons of recipes out there and you will find the ones you like.* **"**
> **—Jason G., 19**

Toward the end of cooking time, add additional salt to taste and sprinkle with pepper. Serve over rice or noodles. Makes 3 or 4 servings.

Laid-back Burger Night Menu

Here's an easy dinner you can share with your friends. Use the burger variations listed in the recipe on page 57 to make custom-seasoned veggie burgers for everyone. You'll have some leftover burger mix: just shape into patties and refrigerate to cook up later in the week (or cook them now and take burgers for lunch).

Menu for Four

Create-Your-Own Veggie Burgers (page 56), served with whole grain buns and favorite burger toppings
  Sesame Slaw (page 109)
  Juice or other beverage
  Freeform Fruit Salad (page 112)

Preparation and Cooking Time: *About 40 minutes to make the whole meal—a little more, a little less, depending on your cooking experience.*

Your Strategy

1. *Make the fruit salad and put it in a bowl in the fridge. This only takes a few minutes; you're basically just cutting up your favorite fruits and tossing them together.*
2. *Soak the textured vegetable protein for the burgers according to the recipe. Meanwhile, chop onion and garlic and get your spices together.*
3. *Move on to the Sesame Slaw. Shred cabbage and grate carrot, or, if using prepackaged coleslaw mix, dump it into a bowl. Mix dressing and add it to slaw and season with salt and pepper. Put in refrigerator until ready to eat.*
4. *Add remaining burger ingredients, mix well, shape into burgers, and cook.*
5. *Serve burgers with buns and toppings, along with the Sesame Slaw, and fruit salad for dessert. Enjoy!*

insanely**easy**

B.J.'s Instant Eggplant Parmesan

Serve these saucy eggplant cubes over pasta. Or spoon over crusty bread, top with melted soy or dairy cheese, and eat as an open-faced sandwich.

½ large eggplant, or 1 smaller eggplant
⅓ cup water
¾ cup store-bought pasta sauce
¼ cup soy or dairy parmesan cheese
  (see note)
2 cups cooked pasta or 2 crusty sandwich
  rolls (optional)

1. Wash eggplant and, leaving the skin on, cut the eggplant into bite-sized cubes (you want about 2 cups total).
2. In a saucepan, boil water, add the eggplant, and cover. Cook for about 5 to 10 minutes, or until eggplant is soft. Drain any remaining water.
3. Add spaghetti sauce, stir, and heat for another minute or so. Add soy or dairy parmesan cheese, stir until combined, and serve over pasta or on a sandwich (or eat plain). Makes 2 servings.

> *"I like to add my own twist to store-bought veggie burgers. I thaw them, mash them up, and then put in my own veggies—things like grated carrots and zucchini. Then I add a little flour and water so that it binds together and reshape them back into patties. You can add seasonings, too. Then, just fry them in a little oil."* **—Patrick, 16**

Note: You could leave the cheese out, or substitute about 2 Tablespoons nutritional yeast flakes; it won't be eggplant "parmesan," but big deal.

Make Your Own Pizza!

Although you can use a store-bought crust, it's fun to make your own pizza dough. And it's not very difficult. Just make sure you give yourself enough time—it takes about an hour for the dough

> 66 *Try all kinds of new foods! You'll never know what you like if you don't experiment.* 99 **—Scott, 17**

to rise. This pizza dough recipe was inspired by Mara, 17. "I like to keep a bag of pizza dough in the fridge and make 'personal pan pizzas' as I please," says Mara. "I top the pizza with whatever I happen to feel like at the time." Once you make the dough, use the recipes on pages 63–65 to inspire your own pizza creations.

Mara's Pizza Dough

> 1 cup warm water (but not hot, more like the temperature of a bath)
> 1 Tablespoon sugar, maple syrup, or honey
> 1 packet (2½ teaspoons) active dry yeast
> 1½ cups whole wheat flour
> 1½ cups unbleached white flour
> 1 teaspoon salt
> 3 Tablespoons olive oil
> Cornmeal for dusting pans
> Extra olive oil for brushing crust

1. Pour warm water into small bowl, add sugar or sweetener, and stir to dissolve. Sprinkle yeast on top of the water and gently stir until yeast is completely dissolved. Let the yeast mixture stand in a warm spot for about 5 minutes, until you see a

> 66 *Volunteering to cook for the whole family is a great idea! Not only is it a way to show your family how good meatless meals can be, the usual chef will be very appreciative of the night off. The best time to volunteer for this is when you have a day off from school, or on a weekend when the rest of the family is very busy. Pick out a recipe a few days before, and include the ingredients on your parents' shopping list. I find that all that time cooking for my family has paid off when I am cooking for all my college housemates, many of whom have never cooked before.* 99 **—Laura, 19**

foamy layer form across the top of the mixture (see note).

2. In a large bowl, combine flours and salt. Scoop a shallow hole in the center of the flour to form a well and pour

> **"**Vegetarian cooking is sooo much easier to clean up after. I've always hated that greasy fat that drips off anything meaty.**"**
> —**Christina, 14**

in the yeast mixture and olive oil. With a big wooden spoon, combine the ingredients until the dough begins to hold together. Add more flour as needed, until the dough pulls away from the sides of the bowl.

3. Turn dough out onto a floured board or countertop and knead for about 8 minutes.

4. Shape the dough into a ball and place it in a well-oiled bowl. Cover tightly with plastic wrap and set in a warm place to rest and rise for about an hour. The dough should double in bulk.

5. When dough is finished rising, knead it lightly for a couple of minutes more and cut into 2 pieces (for making 2 12-inch pizzas; if you want individual-sized pizzas, cut the dough into 4 to 6 pieces).

6. Shape each piece into a ball. With your fingers, flatten each ball into a circle of dough about 6 inches in diameter. Use a rolling pin that has been dusted with flour to roll the dough into a 12-inch pizza crust (6-inch for individual pizzas). Your pizza can be any shape: round, rectangular, whatever.

How to Knead

Kneading is the act of folding, pressing, and turning dough to get it to the right consistency. First, flour your hands. Gather the dough into a mound on the counter or board, lightly dusted with flour, and fold the far side of it toward you. Press on the folded mound of dough with the heels of both hands and push away from you. Turn the dough slightly (so that the folded edge is facing to your side) and repeat the whole process. Add small amounts of flour here and there to keep dough from sticking. Continue the process until the dough is smooth and stretchy, like elastic, about 8 minutes.

> **"**It helps to do some research to support your reasons for being vegetarian. When I first became a vegetarian, I had no clue what I was talking about. I was like, 'Um, I like animals.' Then I became more educated so that I could talk about it. I read about the ways the animals are treated. I don't want to start preaching to anyone. I just want to eat my sandwich. But when people ask me, I tell them what I know. And they start to get interested.**"**
>
> **—Erin, 16**

7. Dust a pizza pan with cornmeal. Transfer pizza crust to pan. Brush the top of the pizza with additional olive oil and top with your favorite toppings (see following suggestions). A pizza baked on this dough will need to bake for 15 to 20 minutes in a 450° F oven.

Note: When mixing yeast, if you don't see a foamy layer after 5 to 10 minutes, it means either that the water is too hot or too cold or that the yeast is inactive. Try again with new yeast and adjust the temperature accordingly.

Hint for even tastier crust: About halfway through the pizza baking time, remove the pizza from the oven (use an oven mitt or pot holders) and brush the crust with more olive oil.

Pizza Possibilities

Try the following topping ideas on either a homemade crust or a store-bought crust.

Veggie Pizza

1. If using Mara's Pizza Dough (page 61), preheat oven to 450° F; if using other crust, read package instructions.

2. Spread **12-inch pizza crust** with **1 cup store-bought pasta or pizza sauce.**

3. Top with ¾ **cup grated soy or dairy mozzarella cheese** (optional).

4. Top pizza with 1½ **cups favorite veggies** (such as sliced onion, mushrooms, green pepper, zucchini, chopped spinach, broccoli, artichoke hearts, or fresh garlic).

5. Sprinkle with ¼ **cup or so additional cheese,** if using. If you're not using cheese, it's a good idea to top the pizza with an ingredient that has lots of moisture, like fresh tomato, to keep it from drying out, or use a little extra sauce.

6. Bake according to Mara's Pizza Dough directions or crust package directions.

Mexican Pizza

1. If using Mara's Pizza Dough (page 61), preheat oven to 450° F; if using other crust, follow package instructions.

2. Drain **2 cups salsa** through a strainer to remove excess liquid.

3. Spread salsa over a **12-inch pizza crust.**

4. In a bowl, combine ¾ **cup cooked or canned black beans** (drained and rinsed), ½ **cup frozen corn kernels,** and **2 Table-**

Fresh Garlic and Ginger

Lots of recipes in this book call for fresh garlic and ginger, which you can find at any supermarket. You can use garlic or ginger powder in any recipe, but the fresh stuff tastes so much better. (In general, ⅓ to ½ teaspoon powdered garlic or ginger equals 1 Tablespoon fresh; the same dried-to-fresh equivalent applies to other herbs and seasonings.)

*Fresh **garlic** gives a flavor that can't be beat, especially when sautéed in olive oil at the beginning of a recipe. Garlic comes in bulbs; each bulb is made up of individual cloves of garlic. You have to peel the skin off the garlic (it can help to carefully smash the clove first with the flat side of a blunt knife); then finely chop the clove (this is also called mincing), or put the clove in a garlic press and squeeze. You can also buy bottles of preminced garlic. A note about cooking garlic and onions in the same recipe: because chopped garlic browns more quickly than chopped onion, you will usually add it after the onion has been sautéed.*

*Fresh **ginger root** has a warm zing to it. It's especially good in Asian and Indian food. To use, peel the outer skin and finely chop a bit of the root (it can be a little stringy and tough sometimes, so chop carefully). You can also use the fine part of a grater.*

> **❝** *For pizza, in addition to veggies and stuff, here's a great topping. Thoroughly mash up the following: One teaspoon of nutritional yeast, one half block of tofu, one teaspoon olive oil, a tiny bit of oregano and basil, and pepper, garlic powder, and salt to taste.***❞** —**Tovah, 17**

spoons chopped fresh cilantro. Spread bean topping over pizza.

5. Top with ½ **cup grated pepper jack soy or dairy cheese** (optional).

6. Bake pizza according to Mara's Pizza Dough directions or crust package directions. If not using cheese, garnish the baked pizza with ½ **cup avocado** or **tomato slices** (optional).

Greek Pizza

1. If using Mara's Pizza Dough (page 61), preheat oven to 450° F; if using other crust, follow package instructions.

2. Top **12-inch pizza crust** with ¾ **cup bottled pasta or pizza sauce** (optional—this pizza is great even without sauce).

3. Top with ¼ **cup each of the following:** sliced black olives, sliced bottled or canned artichoke hearts, sliced red onion, sliced fresh mushrooms, and crumbled feta cheese or firm tofu. Top with a few **fresh tomato slices.**

4. Bake pizza according to Mara's Pizza Dough directions or crust package directions.

Broccoli Pesto Calzones

Use your homemade pizza dough to make calzones—stuffed pizza pockets.

Cornmeal for dusting
½ pizza dough recipe (page 61), rolled into
    2 large or 4 small circles
Olive oil for brushing crust
¼ to ½ cup bottled or homemade pesto
    (page 92)

2 cups frozen broccoli florets
1 cup grated soy or dairy mozzarella cheese
 (or crumbled firm tofu)
1 cup bottled pasta sauce
½ cup pine nuts (optional)
⅛ teaspoon crushed red pepper
 flakes (optional)
Dried or fresh basil for garnish

1. Preheat oven to 450° F. Dust a baking pan with cornmeal and place dough circles on baking pan. Brush dough with olive oil.
2. Spread a thin layer of pesto on entire crust, except edges.
3. In a bowl, combine remaining ingredients, except basil, to make the filling. Place the filling on half of each dough circle, dividing filling among the calzones.
4. Form the calzone by lifting the uncovered half of the dough and folding it over the filled side, pressing the clean edges firmly together. Roll the edge to make a seal. Brush the calzones with olive oil, make a few small air slits on each with a knife, and bake for 15 to 20 minutes, or until crust is golden brown. Brush with olive oil halfway through the baking.
5. When calzones are finished, sprinkle with basil as a garnish and let sit for a few minutes before serving. Makes 2 large or 4 smaller calzones.

Grilled Teriyaki Tofu and Veggie Kebabs
Try these at your next cookout. If you have time, marinate all the veggie pieces in the sauce for about ½ hour before assembling the kebabs. You'll need some skewers for these. (Don't use soft or aseptic-packed tofu; it will fall apart on the skewers.)

16 ounce package extra-firm water-packed
 tofu, drained and pressed and cut into
 1½-inch cubes (see page 176 for pressing
 directions)
½ red bell pepper, cut into big chunky pieces

½ green bell pepper, cut into big chunky pieces
Some large mushrooms
Cloves of garlic, peeled (it gets sweet when
    grilled)
1 small zucchini or yellow squash, thickly
    sliced
1 medium onion, cut into chunks
1 cup or so bottled teriyaki sauce (available
    in supermarkets) or other favorite meat-
    free marinade

On the Grill

Most people think "barbecue" means burgers and ribs, but actually, a cookout is one of the easiest vegetarian meals to plan. "When my family is barbecuing hamburgers or hot dogs, I get the fake version of that and eat it alongside them," says Julia, 14. Shish kebabs are easy to make, too.

1. Make kebabs by placing the tofu and vegetable pieces on the skewers, alternating them in whatever pattern you like.
2. Brush the tofu and veggie chunks with a heavy coating of sauce or marinade.
3. Place skewers on the grill. Turn occasionally and grill until slightly charred, about 10 minutes. Brush with additional marinade once or twice while grilling. Makes about 4 to 6 servings.

Note: To eat, remove the veggies and tofu from the skewer. You can use the tofu and veggies as a sandwich filling or just eat them on their own.

Annie's Easy Risotto

Risotto (pronounce ri-SOE-toe) is a traditional Italian rice dish. Risotto is usually cooked on the top of the stove, but it's easier to bake it in the oven.

1 Tablespoon olive oil
1 small onion, finely chopped
1 or 2 cloves garlic, peeled and finely chopped
1 cup arborio rice (a chewy rice available in

supermarkets) or regular white rice
2 cups vegetable broth (canned is fine)
2½ to 3 cups frozen chopped spinach
½ cup finely chopped mushrooms
1 medium tomato, diced
½ cup soy or dairy parmesan cheese
(optional, see note)

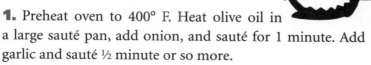

1. Preheat oven to 400° F. Heat olive oil in a large sauté pan, add onion, and sauté for 1 minute. Add garlic and sauté ½ minute or so more.

2. Add rice and stir to coat. Add broth and bring to a boil. Stir in spinach, mushrooms, tomatoes, and ¼ cup of the soy or dairy cheese, if using.

3. Pour into an oiled casserole dish, top with remaining cheese if using, cover, and bake for 35 to 40 minutes or until most of the liquid is gone and rice is tender. Serves 4 to 6.

Note: If you want to make this without cheese, add ¼ **teaspoon** or so extra **salt,** plus **1 Tablespoon margarine.** If you have any on hand, stir in ¼ **cup nutritional yeast** to make it taste cheesy. It really works!

Some Barbecue Tips

■ *Be creative: You can grill thick slices of eggplant, zucchini, carrots, peppers, or whatever vegetables you like.*

■ *For easy corn on the cob, remove husks and silk, wrap the ears in heavy aluminum foil, and lay them on top of coals. Cook about 10 minutes, turning occasionally.*

■ *Ask for a meat-free part of the grill, or cover the grill with a bit of foil.*

■ *Cook veggie burgers and dogs for just a few minutes to avoid drying them out. You can also brush them with barbecue sauce or teriyaki sauce or spritz them with water.*

■ *For delicious roasted potatoes, mix together a combination of* **new potatoes** *(they're the small red ones),* **whole garlic cloves** *(peeled), a drizzle of* **olive oil,** *some* **rosemary,** *and* **salt and pepper.** *Wrap in foil and place on grill for about 30 minutes, or place foil package directly on coals and check in about 20 minutes.*

insanely**easy**

Vegetable Couscous Marinara

1 cup water or vegetable broth
½ cup frozen broccoli florets
½ cup chopped red bell pepper
1 scallion, finely chopped

Easy Meal Planning Tips

1. *Check out what the rest of your family is eating.* You may be able to use some of their ingredients in your own vegetarian dishes. If your mom or dad is making a stir-fry with vegetables and chicken, for example, you can use the same vegetables but add tofu instead. Some family favorites can easily be made vegetarian. "My mom has this great casserole recipe. It usually contains meat, but I get my own special one made with tofu," says Amy, 16.

2. *Keep cooked grains and chopped veggies on hand.* If you're making pasta or rice, cook some extra and store it in the refrigerator for the next meal. When you're chopping onions and carrots for tonight's lentil soup, chop extra for tomorrow's stir-fry. No big deal.

3. *Think of leftovers as your friend.* Tonight's meal can also be tomorrow's lunch. "I sometimes make enough so that I can freeze the leftovers," says Mara, 17. It's nice to have something to throw in the microwave on days when you have no time at all to cook. If you're tired of your leftovers, change them: Add noodles to leftover chili. Use a stew as a sauce over rice. Use a salad to stuff pita pockets.

4. *Keep a few convenience foods on hand.* "If I have enough time, I cook things from scratch, but when I'm in a rush, I use packaged things and add a little of my own creativity to spice it up a bit," says Julia, 14. Store-bought pizza crusts, veggie burgers, canned chili, and frozen stir-fry mixes are good things to stash.

5. *Get out of the meat-as-main-course mode.* "It's very helpful to change the way you think about food," says Jason G., 19. "You're not simply trying to replace the meat." No longer are vegetables second-class citizens; experiment with recipes that put veggies, whole grains, beans, and other vegetarian foods at the center of your plate. Well-planned vegetarian meals are super-nutritious and very filling.

1 Tablespoon olive oil

¼ teaspoon salt

¾ cup couscous

¾ cup cooked or canned chickpeas, drained

¼ cup raisins

¼ cup slivered almonds (if you want, you
can toast them first; see Easy Homemade
Granola, page 13)

Squirt of fresh lemon juice

½ teaspoon dried mint or basil (optional)

Salt and pepper to taste

2 cups bottled marinara pasta sauce, warmed
in microwave or on stovetop

1. Pour water or broth in a medium saucepan and add broccoli, pepper, scallion, olive oil, and salt. Bring to a boil.

2. Turn off heat and add couscous and chickpeas. Cover and let
sit for 15 minutes, or until couscous has absorbed water.

3. Add remaining ingredients and stir to combine. Spoon onto
plates or into bowls and top each serving with warm marinara
sauce. Serves 4.

insanely**easy**

Southern Chili

*There are as many variations on chili as there are people who
cook it. This one is a little unusual and absolutely easy. The okra,
corn, and hominy (a type of big, white, chewy corn, available
in the Mexican or canned
vegetable section of the supermarket) give it the flavor of
the Deep South. A serrano or
jalapeño chili pepper gives it
zing. If you can find organic
canned tomatoes and tomato
paste, they'll make this dish
even better. No lie.*

> **"**I choose not to eat meat, flesh, or what-
> ever you want to call it, and other people
> choose to eat it. I want people to respect
> my decision and to allow me to eat what
> I want without being hassled for it. So, I
> treat those who do eat meat with the
> same respect.**"**   **—Kathleen, 17**

3 Tablespoons olive oil

1 medium onion, chopped

2 cloves garlic, finely chopped

1 serrano or jalapeño chili pepper,
   finely chopped (see page 50)

1½ to 2 teaspoons cumin

¼ teaspoon finely ground red chili powder or
   cayenne pepper

15 ounce can pinto beans,
   black beans, or kidney
   beans, drained

28 ounce can diced tomatoes,
   with liquid

6 ounce can tomato paste

1 cup canned white hominy, drained

¾ cup frozen corn kernels

¾ cup frozen okra slices

2 Tablespoons chopped fresh cilantro
   (optional)

Any Bean Will Do

You can jazz up any kind of plain canned beans in no time at all: just dump them into a saucepan, add some **chopped garlic** *and* **onion** *(or* **garlic powder** *and* **onion powder**)*,* **cumin, chili powder, hot sauce,** *and a little* **water***. Or, even simpler, add* **salsa** *to* **canned beans** *and heat. To turn it into a meal, toss in some* **frozen vegetables** *(green beans, peppers) or a handful of* **chopped fresh vegetables** *(use anything in the fridge that looks like it needs to be used right now), simmer for 8 to 10 minutes, add some* **chopped fresh cilantro,** *and serve over* **cooked rice.**

---

1. Heat oil in a large, deep pan over medium heat. Add onion, garlic, and jalapeño chili and sauté for 1 to 2 minutes, but don't let garlic turn brown.

2. Add cumin, beans, tomatoes, tomato paste, hominy, corn, and okra. Stir to combine. Cook for about 15 minutes or a little longer, stirring occasionally, until mixture is well heated and flavors are blended. Serve in bowls and top with cilantro, if desired. Makes about 6 servings.

Variation: Serve chili over **macaroni** or **couscous.**

Chili Dinner Menu

Your whole family will enjoy this chili dinner, and you'll love how fast and easy it is to make. Feel free to add your favorite vegetables and spices to the chili—if you like spicy food, make it as hot as you can handle! The leftovers will be perfect for your school lunch (chili tastes even better the next day, because the flavors have had a chance to blend).

Menu for Four:

Southern Chili (page 70)
Cornbread or Cornbread Muffins (pages 147–48) with
Seasoned Spread (page 140)
  Juice or other beverage
  Lemon or berry sorbet

Preparation and Cooking Time: *About 45 minutes—a little more, a little less, depending on your cooking experience*

Your Strategy

1. *Make cornbread or cornbread muffins according to the recipe. The cornbread will probably be finished before you're finished with the chili, but that's good, because it should cool a bit before you cut it.*
2. *Make the chili according to the recipe.*
3. *Prepare Seasoned Spread according to the recipe.*
4. *When chili is ready, serve with big slices of cornbread spread with Seasoned Spread. Pour beverages. Serve scoops of sorbet for dessert.*

insanely**easy**

No-Brainer Bean and Green Wraps

This is a great recipe for days when you're too busy to think about what to make. It's really fast and very filling.

  1 can pinto beans, white beans, or black
    beans, with liquid
  1 or 2 cloves garlic, peeled and finely
    chopped

1 teaspoon ground cumin
1 teaspoon ground coriander
2 cups chopped collard greens or kale (if you want to skip the chopping, use frozen greens)
Small handful fresh cilantro (optional)
4 to 6 corn tortillas
Your favorite toppings: hot sauce, avocado slices, chopped tomato, grated soy or dairy cheese

1. Dump the beans, liquid and all, into a large skillet and add the chopped garlic and the cumin and coriander. Heat on medium heat for about 2 or 3 minutes. While the beans are heating, chop the greens and cilantro (if using).

2. Add the greens and cilantro to the beans and cover the pan with a lid. (If the liquid from the beans looks like it has cooked away, add a few tablespoons of water before adding greens.) Cook only until the greens are steamed—about 1½ or 2 minutes. While it's cooking, warm the tortillas in the microwave for 30 to 45 seconds or in the toaster oven for about 1 minute.

3. Spoon bean and green filling onto warm tortillas and add toppings of choice. Fold up and eat. Serves 2 to 4, depending on how hungry you are.

Try Portobello Mushrooms!

Portobello mushrooms have big, flat, meaty caps. They even taste a little meatlike. You can find portobellos in most supermarkets. They seem expensive if you look at the price per pound, but three or four mushrooms don't weigh a lot, so it doesn't add up to much.

*To make **Portobello Mushroom Fajitas**, slice the mushroom caps into thick pieces and use instead of seitan in the recipe on page 74.*

*To make **Portobello Mushroom Burgers**: marinate the mushroom cap for 10 minutes or longer in a mixture of a little **olive oil**, a little **tamari or soy sauce**, garlic, and **balsamic or apple cider vinegar**. Broil for about 5 to 7 minutes on each side, or until browned. Serve on a bun with toppings.*

Sweet and Spicy Seitan Fajitas

Seitan is a very meatlike food; read about it on page 174.

4 corn or flour tortillas
1 Tablespoon olive oil
½ cup sliced onion
⅛ to ¼ teaspoon red chili flakes, depending
    on how hot you like it
1 clove garlic, peeled and chopped
½ cup chopped green pepper pieces
1 cup seitan pieces
1 Tablespoon tamari or soy sauce
2 Tablespoons water
½ teaspoon molasses or 1 teaspoon orange or
    apple juice concentrate
Splash of apple cider vinegar

1. Wrap tortillas in foil and place in 300° F oven or toaster oven to heat while preparing the fajita filling. You can also warm them in a microwave for 45 seconds on high setting. (Don't wrap in foil if using the microwave—just put them on a plate.)
2. Heat oil in a large skillet, and add the onion. After about a minute, add the red chili flakes, and sauté together until onion starts to brown. Add garlic and sauté just about 1 minute more (don't let the garlic turn brown).
3. Add green pepper pieces, stir, add the seitan pieces, mix together, and cook for 1 minute. Add the tamari or soy sauce, water, and molasses or juice concentrate, and then mix togeth-

> **"***I'm vegan for ethical reasons, because I don't believe that human animals are above non-human animals and [I believe] that we don't have the right to use animals as we wish. I feel very strongly about this. I would've been vegan a lot earlier if I had known the harm that milk production does to cows. I also won't wear leather, silk, wool, or makeup that comes from animals. People think of vegans as frail, weak, and malnourished, but I'm strong and I dance and I'm on varsity track, so I think that's an untrue stereotype.***"**   **—Anina, 15**

> **"**Don't be afraid to try new vegetarian foods. They may sound strange, but most are delicious!**"**   —Julia, 14

er, cover, and let cook for about 5 minutes.

4. Just at the end of cooking time, add the splash of apple cider vinegar, and mix together.

Spoon the mixture into the tortillas, wrap, and eat. Serves 2 to 4.

Variation: For **Veggie Fajitas,** substitute **2 cups sliced vegetables** for the seitan (you use more veggies because they will shrink some). Try green and red bell peppers, zucchini or yellow squash, and tomato. Add some cubes of tofu for extra protein, if you'd like.

Tofu Rancheros Tostadas

15 ounce can vegetarian refried beans
1½ Tablespoons vegetable or olive oil
½ cup chopped onion
½ cup chopped green pepper
12 ounces firm or extra-firm tofu,
    drained and cubed (or crumbled)
Salt and pepper to taste
Dash of cumin (optional)
4 to 6 tostada shells
Salsa for topping

1. Heat the refried beans in a small saucepan for about 3 minutes or in a bowl in the microwave for about 2 minutes on high setting.

2. Meanwhile, heat oil in a skillet, add onion and green pepper, and sauté for 1 minute.

3. Add tofu and sauté for about 4 minutes, stirring often, until tofu starts to brown. Sprinkle in salt and pepper and cumin, if using.

4. Heat tostada shells in toaster oven for about a minute (heating isn't necessary, but it's a nice touch). You can also heat them in a microwave for about 45 seconds on high setting or in a 300° F oven for about 10 minutes. Spread tostada shell with a layer of refried beans, top with tofu topping and salsa, and serve. Makes 4 to 6 tostadas.

Variation: For **Bean and Burger Tostadas,** omit the refried beans and tofu from the recipe. Instead, add a **15 ounce can whole black or pinto beans** (drained and rinsed) to the sautéed onion and green pepper, along with **2 chopped store-bought veggie burgers.** Season as above and cook for a few minutes until thoroughly heated.

insanely**easy**

Aztec Casserole

An instant Mexican dinner with very little clean-up. Mix the ingredients and throw the casserole into the oven when you get home from school, and you'll be eating in no time.

15 ounce can black beans, drained
15 ounce can diced tomatoes
1 cup salsa
1 cup frozen corn kernels
½ teaspoon cumin
Salt to taste

1½ cups grated Monterey jack or cheddar-style
   soy cheese or dairy cheese—or use crumbled
   soft tofu combined with a little salsa
8 to 12 corn tortillas
Avocado slices

1. Preheat oven to 400° F. Lightly oil a medium-sized casserole dish.

2. In a large bowl, combine beans, tomatoes, salsa, corn, cumin, and salt.

3. Place a layer of 4 to 6 tortillas to cover the bottom of the casserole dish, overlapping the edges. Cover tortilla layer with half of the beans and half of the cheese or tofu, then repeat the layering until all ingredients are used. Bake for about 20 minutes. Remove casserole, cover, and let cool for at least 15 minutes before serving.

Build Your Own Burrito

Take a tortilla, a little of this, a little of that, and you've got yourself a burrito. Use this chart as a guideline, but feel free to add whatever sounds good!

Wrapper	Filling	Veggies	Topping
Select 1 from this column; warm before filling	*Select 1 or more*	*Select 2 or more*	*Select 1 or more*
Whole wheat flour tortilla White flour tortilla Corn tortilla Specialty tortilla (spinach or other flavor)*	Canned black beans or pinto beans (heated) Canned vegetarian refried beans (heated) Tofu or tempeh slices sautéed in oil with garlic, onion, and tamari or soy sauce Grated soy or dairy cheese (Monterey, jalapeño jack, or cheddar), melted onto tortilla	Grated carrots Chopped zucchini Shredded lettuce or sprouts Chopped tomato Chopped onion or scallion Corn kernels Chopped broccoli Sliced mushroom Avocado slices	Guacamole (page 50) Salsa (bottled or homemade, pages 48–50) Tofu sour cream (page 51) or dairy sour cream Hot sauce Chopped cilantro

Available at natural foods stores and some supermarkets

Kathleen's Veggie Tacos

This recipe is from 17-year-old Kathleen. "My family cooks traditional Mexican food," says Kathleen. "I'm the only veg in my whole family, and they usually won't even touch my food, but they love these tacos."

> 2 Tablespoons vegetable or olive oil
> 2 potatoes, shredded (use a hand grater or food processor)
> ½ or so medium zucchini, shredded
> 1 teaspoon vegetable-herb seasoning blend (available in supermarkets and natural foods stores)
> Salt and pepper to taste
> ½ cup shredded soy or dairy mozzarella cheese (or use crumbled tofu)
> 4 to 6 taco shells
> Favorite toppings, such as salsa, chopped tomato, onion, lettuce, and avocado

1. Heat oil in a large sauté pan and lightly fry potatoes and zucchini until they start to turn golden brown.
2. Add seasonings and cheese or tofu and continue frying until mixture is slightly crispy. Spoon into taco shells and serve with your favorite toppings. Makes 4 to 6 tacos.

---

insanely easy

Fastest Taco Filling in Town
*Heat a little **oil** in a pan, sauté some **vegetarian "ground beef" crumbles** (available in the frozen foods section of natural foods stores and some supermarkets), and add **prepackaged taco seasoning mix.** Serve with your favorite toppings. (It's a great solution when the rest of the family is eating meat tacos for dinner.)*

Vegetable Fried Rice with Tofu

Turn your kitchen into a Chinese restaurant. This is a good recipe for using leftover rice. For a speedier version, use 1½ cups frozen stir-fry vegetable blend instead of the fresh chopped veggies.

2 Tablespoons tamari or soy sauce

5 Tablespoons water

1 teaspoon fresh ginger root, peeled and
chopped (see page 64), or ¾ teaspoon
ground ginger

1½ teaspoons apple juice concentrate or
1 teaspoon sugar

1 Tablespoon vegetable oil combined with
1 Tablespoon sesame oil

2 scallions, chopped

¾ cup extra firm tofu in ½ inch cubes

Pinch of cayenne pepper or crushed red
pepper flakes (optional)

1½ cups of your favorite veggies, finely chopped
(try a mix of cauliflower, carrot, mushrooms,
and broccoli) and frozen green peas

2 cups cooked brown rice (use leftovers or
see page 115 for directions)

1 teaspoon apple cider vinegar or rice vinegar

1. In a small bowl, mix together tamari or soy sauce, water, ginger, and fruit concentrate or sugar and set aside.

2. In a large skillet or sauté pan, heat oils and add scallion. Sauté for a minute or so, add tofu cubes and about 2 teaspoons of the tamari-ginger mixture, stir, and cook for about 2 minutes. Add cayenne pepper or crushed red pepper flakes, if using.

3. Add veggies, stir, cover, and cook about 2 minutes more. Add rice and remaining tamari-ginger mixture, stir, continue to cook for 2 or 3 minutes, until liquid is absorbed and flavors seem blended.

4. Add vinegar, stir, and taste; add a little extra tamari or soy sauce or other seasonings if you think it needs it. Serves about 4.

Rice Hints

For fast brown rice, you can use the instant kind. It's available in supermarkets and cooks in about 10 minutes. The texture is a little different from regular brown rice, but it'll do. You can also use white rice in any of these dishes if you'd like. For a real treat, try basmati rice—it has a nutty, flowery aroma.

Beth's Rainbow Veggie Stir-Fry with Tofu

It's cooking by color: experiment with your favorite vegetables to get the look and taste you want.

> 1 cup uncooked brown rice or 8 ounces pasta
> ½ pound extra-firm tofu, drained and pressed (see page 176 for pressing instructions)
> 2 Tablespoons tamari or soy sauce
> 2 Tablespoons Szechwan sauce (available in supermarkets; taste first and adjust amount, because some brands are hotter than others)
> 2 or 3 cloves garlic, peeled and finely chopped
> 1 Tablespoon fresh ginger root, peeled and chopped
> 2½ Tablespoons oil (a combination of vegetable oil and sesame oil is good)
>
> *The Veggies:*
> > ½ cup something orange: sliced carrots, orange bell pepper
> > ½ cup something yellow: canned baby corn, sliced yellow bell pepper, yellow squash
> > ½ cup something green: trimmed snow peas, broccoli florets and stalks, asparagus
> > ½ cup something red: chopped red bell pepper, diced tomato
> > ½ cup something white: sliced or whole water chestnuts, sliced fresh mushrooms, chopped onion
>
> Sesame seeds for garnish

1. Cook rice (page 115) or pasta (page 90) according to directions.

2. Meanwhile, make marinade: mix tamari or soy sauce, Szechwan sauce, garlic, and ginger in a small bowl. Set aside.

3. When tofu is finished draining, cut into bite-sized cubes,

> **"**Be creative, and learn your spices. When I'm cooking, I'll spontaneously think, 'Hmm, sage sounds good,' or something like that, and it usually works. (It's best to add a little at a time; if a little is good, a lot is not always better.)**"**
> —**Johanna, 19**

place in bowl, and pour about half the marinade over it. Gently mix and let the tofu sit for about 10 minutes.

4. When the tofu is finished marinating, heat about 1 Tablespoon of the oil in a large skillet or wok. When oil is hot but not smoking, carefully add the tofu and its marinade. Stir-fry for a few minutes, until tofu is heated through. Remove tofu and set aside.

5. Heat remaining oil in the pan, add veggies and remaining marinade. Cook for about 3 or 4 minutes, stirring often. The vegetables should contact the bottom of the pan; if there are too many vegetables for this to happen, cover the pan to keep the heat in while cooking and remove the cover occasionally to stir. When the veggies are almost done, add tofu, stir, cover, and cook for about 2 minutes more.

6. Serve over rice or pasta, sprinkle with sesame seeds, and drizzle with extra tamari or soy sauce, if desired. Serves 4.

Crunchy Greens Stir-Fry

Bok choy is a type of Chinese cabbage that's loaded with calcium; it's available in supermarkets. It has a surprisingly sweet flavor, and the white part of each stalk has lots of crunch.

1 cup uncooked brown or white rice (about
    3 cups cooked rice)
2 Tablespoons olive oil
3 scallions, chopped
2 cloves garlic, peeled and finely chopped
3 carrots, thinly sliced
½ pound tofu, drained and pressed (see
    page 176 for pressing instructions) and
    cut into cubes
1 Tablespoon tamari or soy sauce

6 to 8 bok choy leaves (including the white stalk), chopped
½ teaspoon hot sauce (optional)
½ teaspoon black pepper
Splash of rice vinegar (optional, but really good)
Sprinkle of sesame seeds (optional)

1. Cook rice according to directions on page 115.

2. Meanwhile, heat oil in a large skillet. Add scallions and carrots, cover, and sauté for about 2 minutes. Add garlic and sauté for 1 more minute.

3. Add cubed tofu. Stir to coat the tofu with oil. Add tamari or soy sauce, cover, and cook for about 5 minutes, stirring occasionally to brown tofu lightly on all sides.

4. Add bok choy leaves and stalks and cover. Cook about 2 or 3 minutes, until bok choy leaves are steamed but not overcooked.

5. Add hot sauce, if using, and pepper. Add more tamari or soy sauce (or salt) to taste. Add splash of rice vinegar, and sprinkle with sesame seeds, if using. Serve over rice. Makes 2 to 4 servings.

For a Fast, Light Meal, Stuff a Potato

*Kim, 17, of Idaho, suggests **Stuffed Greek Potatoes**: Slice the side off a **baked potato**, scoop out the insides and scrape the potato from the cut side, and combine the potato with **crumbled feta cheese or firm tofu**, **onion powder** or finely chopped **onion**, a little **soymilk** or other milk, **salt**, **pepper**, and **oregano**. Place the filling back in the potato, top with more crumbled feta or tofu, drizzle with a little **olive oil**, and place the potato under the broiler for about 10 minutes (watch the potatoes so they don't get too browned). "I have lots of great potato recipes, because my father is a potato farmer," says Kim. "Yahoo for spuds!" Try creating your own potato fillings with grilled tempeh or tofu pieces, pesto sauce, or steamed veggies.*

Indian Chickpea Masala

Enter the spicy world of Indian cuisine! A few of the spices may sound unusual, but they're easy to find and easy to use. You'll find ground cardamom and coriander in the spice aisle of the super-market. Serve this over cooked rice or with warm flat bread.

3½ Tablespoons vegetable oil
1 large onion, finely chopped (about 2 cups)
4 cloves garlic, peeled and finely
   chopped
2 Tablespoons fresh ginger root,
   peeled and finely chopped
Spices:
   2 teaspoons ground cardamom
   1 teaspoon ground coriander
   ¼ teaspoon black pepper
   ¼ teaspoon salt
¾ cup finely chopped canned or
   fresh tomato
Juice of ½ lemon
2 15 ounce cans chickpeas (or
   1 28 ounce can) with liquid drained into a
   small bowl and set aside

1. Heat oil in a large saucepan or sauté pan, add onions, and sauté for about 3 minutes, stirring often. Add garlic and ginger, stir, and sauté for 3 more minutes, stirring often.

2. Combine all spices and add to onions and garlic. Immediately add tomatoes and lemon juice. Cook for about 5 minutes, stirring often to prevent sticking. Add chickpea liquid, lower heat, and simmer for 10 minutes.

3. Add chickpeas and cook for 10 minutes more. Serve over rice or with flat bread. Serves about 6.

> **"**I don't know why people think cooking without meat is such a big deal. I think it's far worse to cook with meat, because to me, there is nothing more disgusting than a big piece of raw animal.**"**
>
> **—Kim, 17**

Thai Coconut Curry

This dish calls for canned coconut milk, which is a creamy, rich liquid from the inside of coconuts. You can find it in the Asian section of most supermarkets. It adds an exotic flavor to this simple curry. For a complete meal, serve this with Lemony Cukes (page 108) on the side, and Mango Freeze (page 155) for dessert.

½ cup water
1 large potato, cut into 1-inch chunks
3 carrots, peeled and sliced into chunks
    about 1 inch thick
2 Tablespoons vegetable oil
1 medium onion, cut into chunks
2 cloves garlic, peeled and roughly chopped
4 thin slices fresh ginger root (peeled) or
    1 teaspoon dried ground ginger
1½ to 2 teaspoons curry powder
15 ounce can coconut milk
1 Tablespoon tamari or soy sauce
1½ cups broccoli florets and stalks, chopped
¼ cup frozen green peas
1 teaspoon brown sugar or other sweetener
    (optional)
2 teaspoons rice vinegar or lime juice
Salt and pepper to taste
3 or 4 cups cooked brown rice or noodles
    (see brown rice cooking directions,
    page 115)

1. Put water, potatoes, and carrots in a medium-sized saucepan. Cover and cook over medium heat for about 10 minutes, or until vegetables start to get tender.

2. While vegetables are cooking, heat oil in a large saucepan or skillet with high sides. Add onion and sauté for about 2 minutes. Add garlic and ginger and sauté for about 1 minute, but don't let garlic turn brown. Add curry powder, stir, and sauté for about 30 seconds more.

3. Add coconut milk and tamari or soy sauce, cover, and cook for about 5 minutes. Add broccoli and peas, cover, and cook for 2 minutes.

4. Drain water from potatoes and carrots and add to curry mixture. Add brown sugar, if using, and cook for 1 more minute. Add vinegar, salt, and pepper to taste. Serve over rice or noodles. Makes 4 servings.

Variation: Add ½ **pound extra-firm tofu,** cut into 1-inch cubes. Add tofu to the onion/garlic/ginger sauté before adding curry powder and other ingredients.

EASY
PASTA DISHES

"*I mixed everything together. . . . woohoo . . . It was pretty. A good improvement over regular spaghetti.***"**
 —Scott, 17

For a fast, easy meal, cook up some pasta. All you have to do is put a pot of noodles on to cook, and, in the meantime, get your sauce or toppings together. Add a little salad and you've got yourself a dinner.

The great thing about pasta is that it's so versatile. You can eat it with bottled sauce or your own homemade stuff. It can be as easy as noodles tossed with olive oil, garlic, salt, and pepper, or as complex as baked shells stuffed with tofu-vegetable filling. You can make your pasta cheesy or vegan.

The following recipes will give you a starting point, but don't stop here. Noodle around! And remember that pasta is delicious cold, too, so it's good for school lunches. Try some of the pasta salad recipes on pages 109–11.

Try some of the pasta salad recipes on pages 109–11.

insanely**easy**

Peanut Pasta

This easy pasta is good hot or cold, and it's a great transportable lunch food. In a hurry? "I just make a sauce of melted peanut butter and a little water and toss it with my spaghetti," says Anina, 15.

8 ounces of your favorite pasta
½ cup smooth or crunchy peanut butter
¼ cup warm water
2 Tablespoons tamari or soy sauce
1 Tablespoon rice vinegar or lemon juice
1 Tablespoon orange juice concentrate
¼ teaspoon cayenne pepper or crushed red chilies (or more if you like things spicy)

1 clove garlic, peeled and chopped (or
⅟₂ teaspoon garlic powder)
½ to 1 teaspoon fresh chopped ginger root
(or ½ teaspoon dried ground ginger)
¼ cup frozen green peas, thawed
1 finely sliced scallion, white and green part
(optional)
¼ cup grated carrot (optional)

1. Cook pasta according to directions below or package directions.

2. Meanwhile, combine peanut butter, water, tamari or soy sauce, vinegar or lemon juice, orange juice concentrate, cayenne pepper or crushed chilies, garlic, and ginger in a blender or food processor. Blend until smooth and set aside.

Pasta Cooking Basics

To cook dried pasta, bring a large pot of water to a boil. Use 5 quarts of water for 1 pound of pasta. Using plenty of water helps keep the pasta moving around and prevents it from sticking together. If you want, add a little salt, but not until just before you add the pasta. Add the pasta, and boil it until it is tender but still has a bit of firmness to it. For most pastas, 8 to 12 minutes usually does the trick, but it depends on the size and shape of the noodle. It's best to test the pasta to see if it's done; just lift a noodle out of the pot with a large utensil, briefly run it under cold water to cool it down, and bite it to check the texture: it should be tender but firm. Don't overcook your pasta or it will be too soft and mushy. (Fresh pasta cooks in just a few minutes.)

When the pasta is finished, place a large colander in the sink, use pot holders to pick up the pasta pot, and pour the boiling water and noodles into the colander to drain. If you're not ready to mix the noodles with the sauce, put them back in the cooking pot. You can toss them with a little olive oil to prevent them from sticking.

3. About one minute before pasta is finished cooking, add peas, bring back to a boil, and cook for one more minute. When pasta is finished, drain noodles and peas and combine them with the sauce.

4. Add scallion and carrot, if desired. Toss together and serve warm or chilled. Serves 4.

insanely**easy**

Angel Hair with Broccoli

> 8 ounces angel hair pasta
> 5 to 8 cloves garlic, pressed in a garlic press or finely chopped (the more the better—really!)
> 16 ounce bag frozen broccoli pieces (or ½ bag broccoli, ½ bag green beans)
> 3 Tablespoons olive oil
> ¼ cup soy or dairy parmesan cheese (optional, see note)
> ⅛ to ¼ teaspoon black pepper
> ½ to 1 teaspoon salt

1. In a large pot, cook pasta according to package directions or directions on page 90.

2. About halfway through pasta cooking time, add garlic and continue cooking. With about 3 minutes left to pasta cooking time, add broccoli and/or green beans, bring water back to a boil, and cook for 3 more minutes.

3. When pasta is finished cooking, drain pasta and broccoli in a colander over the sink and then dump them back in the pot. Add remaining ingredients and toss together. Adjust the seasonings to suit your taste. Serves 4.

Note: If you omit the cheese, add a dash of **dried basil or oregano** and a little extra **salt** and **pepper**.

Pesto Pasta

Most pesto contains cheese, but this version is vegan. It's delicious warm or cold—great for school lunches. Experiment with different kinds of nuts. Try the pesto on pizza, too.

> 8 ounces of your favorite pasta (a small pasta
>   with lots of nooks to hold the sauce is
>   good, like spiral or radiatore)
> 1 medium-sized bunch (about 2 cups) basil
>   leaves, washed
> 3 large cloves garlic, peeled
> ⅓ to ½ cup walnuts, almonds, or pine nuts
> ½ cup olive oil
> Juice of 1 lemon (about 2 tablespoons)
> ½ teaspoon salt, or to taste
> Black pepper to taste
> 1 chopped tomato (optional)

1. Cook pasta according to package directions or directions on page 90.

2. Meanwhile, remove and discard the stems from basil. In a food processor or blender, combine basil leaves with remaining ingredients, except tomato. Blend until everything is very finely chopped and forms a paste.

3. When pasta is done, drain noodles, let cool for a few minutes, and toss them with the pesto in a large bowl or pasta cooking pot. Toss in tomato, if using, and season with additional salt and pepper. Serve warm or chilled. Serves 2 to 4.

Variation: For a cheese version, add ¼ **cup soy or dairy parmesan cheese** and reduce salt to ¼ teaspoon or less.

Pasta Primavera

If you'd rather not chop, use a frozen vegetable blend instead of the fresh vegetables in this recipe.

> 8 ounces bowtie or radiatore pasta
> ½ cup water for cooking vegetables

2 carrots, sliced

½ cup green beans

⅓ cup peas

½ cup sliced yellow summer squash

½ cup mushrooms

¼ cup sliced red bell pepper

2 Tablespoons dairy-free
   margarine, or olive oil

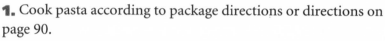

2 scallions, sliced, or ¼ cup chopped onion

2 cloves garlic, peeled and finely chopped

2 Tablespoons flour

1 cup soymilk combined with ½ cup water

1 Tablespoon tamari or soy sauce

1 teaspoon dried basil

¼ teaspoon salt, or to taste

Black pepper to taste

¼ cup soy or dairy parmesan cheese (optional)

1. Cook pasta according to package directions or directions on page 90.

2. Meanwhile, in a small saucepan, bring the ½ cup water to a boil, and add carrots. Cover and simmer for about 2 minutes. Add green beans, peas, yellow squash, mushrooms, and red pepper; cover, and cook the veggies for about 2 minutes, or until they are tender. Pour out any remaining cooking liquid. Keep your eye on the pasta; when the pasta is finished, drain and set aside.

3. To make the sauce, melt margarine or heat oil in a non-stick skillet or large saucepan. Add onion and sauté for about 1 minute; add garlic and sauté about 30 seconds longer. Add flour and stir until margarine or oil is absorbed. Add the soymilk-water combination and stir until smooth. Add tamari or soy sauce. Add

Try All Kinds of Noodles

Try noodles such as Japanese soba, Chinese bean threads, and Thai rice noodles. Look for unusual pasta shapes in the supermarket, or for pasta made from corn, amaranth, kamut, and other interesting grains at the natural foods store.

basil, salt, and pepper and simmer for about 3 or 4 minutes, stirring often, until thickened.

4. Put pasta in a big bowl, top with sauce and veggies. Toss it all together, or leave veggies on top. Add additional salt and pepper to taste. Sprinkle with soy or dairy cheese, if using. Makes 4 servings.

Pasta with Tomatoes, Basil, and Garlic
Fresh basil makes this dish truly delicious.

> 8 ounces linguini or other pasta
> 3 to 4 Tablespoons olive oil
> 3 Tablespoons finely chopped garlic
> ⅔ to ¾ cup chopped fresh basil (remove stems first) or 3 Tablespoons dried basil
> 1½ to 2 cups chopped fresh or canned tomato
> Salt and pepper to taste

1. Cook linguini or pasta according to package directions or directions on page 90.

2. Meanwhile, heat oil until very hot in a large skillet. Add garlic and sauté for 1 or 2 minutes. Add tomato and basil and sauté for 1 or 2 minutes more, stirring often

3. Turn off heat, toss tomato-basil mixture with pasta, add salt and pepper, and serve immediately. Makes 2 to 4 servings.

insanely**easy**

Sun-dried Tomato and Artichoke Pasta
This recipe calls for some unusual ingredients (sun-dried tomatoes, artichoke hearts, balsamic vinegar), but it takes only about 15 minutes to prepare.

> 8 ounces of your favorite pasta
> ¾ cup sun-dried tomatoes (the dry kind in a bag)
> 6 ounce jar marinated artichoke hearts, drained and quartered

1 or 2 cloves garlic, pressed through a garlic
   press or finely chopped

1 teaspoon dried basil

2 Tablespoons olive oil

½ cup canned vegetable broth mixed with 1
   Tablespoon cornstarch

¼ cup soymilk (or use an additional ¼ cup
   broth, but soymilk adds creaminess)

2 teaspoons balsamic vinegar

½ teaspoon salt or to taste

Pepper to taste

Sprinkling of soy or dairy parmesan
   cheese (optional)

1. Cook pasta according to directions on page 90.

2. With 3 minutes left to pasta cooking time, add sun-dried tomatoes. Drain pasta and tomatoes and return to pot.

3. Add artichoke hearts, garlic, basil, olive oil, vegetable broth–cornstarch mixture, and soymilk. Mix together and simmer over medium heat until broth thickens.

4. Add balsamic vinegar and salt and pepper. Remove from heat and serve. Sprinkle with soy or dairy cheese, if using. Serves 4.

Bowties with Tempeh and Mushrooms

12 ounces bowtie pasta

½ 15 ounce can chickpeas,
   plus liquid from can

¼ cup olive oil

½ medium onion, finely chopped

8 ounce package tempeh, cut into ½ inch
   cubes

> **Fast Pasta and Veggies**
>
> *"Here's a super easy way to make pasta even more delicious and nutritious," says Erin, 16. "Cook the noodles for about five minutes. Then add cauliflower and/or broccoli to the cooking noodles, bring the water back to a boil, and cook about five minutes longer. You will get tender noodles and vegetables together!"*

2 cloves garlic, peeled and finely chopped
2 cups sliced mushrooms
1 Tablespoon tamari or soy sauce
½ cup frozen corn
½ cup frozen peas or green beans
Salt and pepper to taste
2 teaspoons apple cider vinegar
 or lemon juice
1 Tablespoon dairy-free
 margarine, or butter
¼ cup soy or dairy parmesan cheese
 (optional)

1. Cook pasta according to directions on page 90.

2. In a small bowl, mash chickpeas. Add chickpea liquid and set aside.

Ruthie's Marinara

Bottled pasta sauce is convenient, but it's fun and easy to make your own. Here's a basic pasta sauce recipe to give you a start:

*1. In a large soup pot or saucepan, heat ⅓ **cup olive oil** over medium heat. Add **3 chopped garlic cloves** and sauté until golden brown. Be careful not to burn the garlic.*

*2. Add **2 28 ounce cans of whole, peeled tomatoes** (organic ones taste best) and crush the tomatoes, using a potato masher or large wooden spoon. Add **1¼ teaspoons dried oregano** and **1½ teaspoons dried basil**, cover, and simmer for at least 45 minutes. If you want, when marinara is finished, add ½ **cup of soy or dairy parmesan cheese**. Add **salt and pepper** to taste. Serve over pasta, on pizza, or in lasagna or other recipes.*

*Variation: If you like **veggies** in your pasta sauce, throw them in after adding garlic. Try adding **chopped onion, green pepper, red pepper, mushrooms, or black olives**. (You can add up to 2 cups of any combination.) For extra protein and a more filling sauce, add ¼ **pound extra-firm tofu**, drained and crumbled.*

3. Heat oil in a large sauté pan, add onion, and sauté for 1 minute. Add tempeh cubes and garlic and sauté, stirring often, until tempeh is lightly browned on all sides. Add mushrooms and sauté for a couple of minutes, stirring occasionally. Add mashed chickpea mixture and tamari or soy sauce and sauté a minute more. Add corn, peas or beans, salt, and pepper and mix together.

4. When pasta is finished cooking, drain and add to tempeh mixture. Stir in vinegar, margarine or butter, and soy or dairy cheese, if using. Makes 4 large servings.

Stuffed Shells

    20 jumbo pasta shells
    1½ cups frozen chopped spinach or broccoli
    8 ounces firm tofu, drained and mashed, or
        1½ cups ricotta or cottage cheese
    26 ounces bottled pasta sauce (select an
        interesting variety, such as garlic and
        herb)
    15 ounce can diced tomatoes
    2 cloves garlic, peeled and very finely
        chopped (or put through garlic
        press)
    ¼ to ½ teaspoon salt (use less if
        using cheese)
    ½ teaspoon dried oregano
    ½ teaspoon dried basil
    ⅓ cup pitted, sliced black olives
        (optional)
    ⅓ cup grated soy or dairy mozzarella or
        parmesan cheese (optional)

1. Cook shells according to package directions. Meanwhile, thaw spinach or broccoli in microwave for about 5 minutes on medium setting. (You can also thaw it by leaving it out for a few

hours before you start cooking.) Squeeze vegetables or pour out excess water. Set aside.

2. Combine tofu or cheese with ½ cup of the pasta sauce, ½ cup of the tomatoes, and all of the spinach or broccoli. Add remaining ingredients except cheese, and combine.

3. When shells are finished cooking, drain water and let shells cool for a couple of minutes before handling. Meanwhile, preheat oven to 350° F and select your baking dish or pan: you can use a 9-inch square or round one or a 9-inch by 13-inch one. (A glass baking dish with a lid is best, but you can also cover the pan with foil.)

4. To assemble shells: spoon some of the pasta sauce on the bottom of the baking dish or pan. Then fill one shell at a time with a spoonful of tofu or cheese mixture and place in pan. If using a smaller baking dish or pan, make two layers; spoon some of the pasta sauce and diced tomatoes over the first layer of shells before adding the second layer. When all shells are in the pan, pour remaining pasta sauce and diced tomatoes over the top. Top with soy or dairy cheese, if desired.

5. Cover pan with lid or foil and bake for 30 minutes. Remove from oven and let sit for 10 to 15 minutes before serving. Serves 4.

Pasta Poetry
by Scott, 17

This isn't really a recipe but I was bored the other day and decided to make myself
some spaghetti; here's what I came up with . . .
I made a bowlful of spaghetti to begin with,
then made some sauce
(extra garlic-y; I love garlic),
opened a can of kidney beans;
chopped up some tofu into little cubes.
Then, after heating the sauce and adding miscellaneous spices,
I mixed everything together.
. . . woohoo . . . It was pretty.
A good improvement over regular spaghetti . . .
lots of protein
and carbohydrates too. . . .

Easy Pasta Dinner Menu

This is a meal you can make in a snap—and the whole family will love it. Here's how:

Menu for Four:

Pasta with Tomatoes, Basil, and Garlic (page 94)
Speediest Side Salad (page 109)
Great Garlic Bread (page 146)
Juice or other beverage
Fruit for dessert

Preparation and Cooking Time: *About 45 minutes to make the whole meal—a little more, a little less, depending on your cooking experience.*

Your Strategy

1. *Put the water for the pasta on to boil. Meanwhile, start with the salad. Wash the salad greens and chop the tomato and cucumber. Assemble the salad, but don't put dressing on yet. Put the salad in a bowl, cover, and place in the refrigerator.*

2. *Chop the garlic, basil, and tomato for the pasta sauce (or just open the can, if you're using canned diced tomato). Chop some extra cloves of garlic for the garlic bread. Keep an eye on the pasta water. When it's boiling, add some salt to the water (optional) and add the noodles. They'll take about 8 to 12 minutes to cook, depending on the type of pasta.*

3. *Preheat the oven for the garlic bread. Spread bread slices with margarine or oil, add garlic, then wrap and bake as directed.*

4. *Keep an eye on the pasta. When it's done, drain it and put it back in the pot. (If it's not done, that's okay, just move on to the next step and keep checking it.)*

5. *Heat oil in a large skillet and prepare the pasta topping as directed in the recipe. When it's done, toss in the drained pasta and combine.*

6. *Remove salad from fridge and add dressing.*

7. *Remove garlic bread from oven (check first to make sure it's done).*

8. *Serve pasta on plates or in pasta bowls. Serve with salad and garlic bread on the side and pour beverage. Serve fruit for dessert.*

insanely**easy**

Lazy Lasagna

Traditionally, lasagna requires that you cook the noodles first before layering them, but this dish uses dry noodles straight out of the box. That means it has a longer baking time (about an hour), but you can throw it together in minutes and then lounge around while it's baking. If you'd rather cut the baking time in half, boil the noodles first.

> 5 cups bottled pasta sauce (almost 2 26 ounce jars)
> 16 ounce box lasagna noodles
> 16 ounce bag frozen spinach, thawed in microwave (or leave it out for a few hours before you start cooking)
> 16 ounce package of extra-firm tofu, drained and crumbled
> 8 to 12 ounce package cheddar or mozzarella soy cheese or dairy cheese, grated
> 1¼ cup boiling water (microwave it or heat it on stovetop)

1. Preheat oven to 350° F. To assemble the lasagna, spread a 9-inch by 12-inch casserole dish or baking pan with ⅓ of the pasta sauce. Then layer remaining ingredients in this order: a layer of noodles, ½ of the spinach, ½ of the tofu, ⅓ of the cheese, another layer of noodles, another ⅓ of the sauce, remaining spinach, remaining tofu, another ⅓ of cheese, another layer of noodles, remaining sauce, remaining cheese.

2. Put the boiling water in a cup with a spout and pour evenly into each corner of the pan so that the water goes to the bottom. Cover the whole pan with aluminum foil and seal the edges all the way around. Place in the oven and bake for 1 hour.

3. Remove foil and check with a fork to see whether noodles are soft all the way through. If not, cover and bake for an additional 10 or 15 minutes. Remove the lasagna from the oven, let sit for about 15 minutes, then serve. Makes 8 to 10 servings.

Note: For the most flavor, choose a pasta sauce with garlic, onions, or other tasty ingredients already added. You can also add ½ **to 1 teaspoon** each **dried oregano** and **basil** to the sauce.

Variation: Use frozen chopped **broccoli** or **zucchini** instead of spinach.

Pasta la Vista

Here's a spicy, colorful pasta with a western attitude; add a slice of cornbread (page 147) to complete your meal. Thanks to my friend Peter for the name of the dish.

8 ounces wagonwheel pasta, elbow macaroni, or other pasta
1 Tablespoon vegetable oil
1 medium onion, chopped
1 to 2 cloves garlic, peeled and finely chopped
½ medium-sized green pepper, chopped
1 stalk celery, thinly sliced
1½ teaspoons cumin
1½ teaspoons paprika
1½ teaspoons oregano
¼ teaspoon salt
¼ teaspoon ground cayenne pepper
15 ounce can diced tomatoes
1½ cups tomato sauce
1 Tablespoon bottled hot sauce
15 ounce can red or pink beans, drained
½ cup frozen corn kernels
Grated soy or dairy cheddar cheese for topping (optional)

1. Cook pasta according to package directions or directions on page 90. While pasta is cooking, heat oil in a large saucepan, add onion, garlic, green pepper, and celery, and sauté for about 5 minutes or until ingredients start to soften.

2. Add all spices to vegetable mixture and stir to combine. Add diced tomatoes, tomato sauce, and hot sauce. Stir to combine and simmer uncovered over medium heat for about 20 minutes.
3. While the sauce is simmering, drain the pasta and set aside. Add beans and corn to the sauce and cook 5 to 10 minutes more. Add the cooked pasta, stir and simmer to heat through. Makes about 6 servings.

---

insanely**easy**

Pasta Caponata

Here's a free-form pasta recipe from Joseph, 18. "I don't really measure things or time everything. I just put the water on to boil for the pasta and start making the sauce. I add the ingredients to the sauce as I chop them. Everything is pretty much finished by the time the pasta is cooked." Adjust ingredient amounts depending on how much you want to make.

*Here's how to do it: Put water on to boil in a large pot and add some **pasta** when water is ready. "I like to use bowties or penne," says Joseph. Meanwhile, to make the sauce, put a little **olive oil** in a large saucepan, add **one or two chopped onions**, a **large can of whole tomatoes** (chop them first, and include liquid), some **dried basil**, a **jar of marinated artichoke hearts** (chopped, with liquid), a **small can of tomato paste**, and about ½ **eggplant**, cut into small cubes (leave skin on). Add more **dried basil** throughout cooking, and maybe a little **salt and pepper** at the end. Cook until the eggplant is soft, and serve over cooked pasta. "If you don't like eggplant," says Joseph, "you can leave it out."*

SALADS

❝The first thing you have to do is disregard any definition of what a salad is.❞   **—Tovah, 17**

When you first told people you were a vegetarian, chances are everyone asked you, "So what do you eat . . . salad?" Of course, vegetarians eat much more than salad. But salads are so easy, so delicious, and so nutritious, you'll want to learn how to make at least a few different kinds.

"The first thing you have to do is disregard any definition of what a salad is," says Tovah, 17. "A salad is not merely a couple of pieces of limp white iceberg lettuce with some slices of cucumber on it." Perhaps more than any other dish, making a salad should be spontaneous. Here are a few suggestions to inspire your own creations.

Garlic Artichoke Salad

This innocent-looking little salad packs a lot of flavor.

1 head romaine lettuce leaves, torn into
   small pieces
½ cup canned artichoke hearts, drained
   and chopped
¼ cup thinly sliced red or white onion
   (about ⅓ of a medium-sized onion)
1½ Tablespoons fresh lemon juice
2 to 3 Tablespoons olive oil
1½ Tablespoons water
1 to 2 cloves fresh garlic, pressed in a garlic
   press or finely chopped
Salt and pepper to taste

1. Wash and drain romaine lettuce leaves. If you have a salad spinner, spin the leaves dry. Place lettuce in a large bowl and add artichoke hearts and onion slices.
2. In a small bowl, combine remaining ingredients and stir vig-

orously (or pour into a small bottle and shake). Taste dressing, adjust salt and pepper, pour over salad. Toss and serve. Serves 4.

Variation: For **Greek Salad,** add **sliced black olives** and little cubes of **feta cheese.**

Sunflower Crunch Salad
Feel free to substitute any of your favorite veggies in this salad.

> 1 head romaine lettuce leaves, torn into
>   small pieces (about 5 to 6 cups)
> ½ cup finely chopped cauliflower
>   and/or broccoli bits
> ¼ cup sliced green pepper
> ¼ cup sliced carrot
> ¼ cup thinly sliced red onion (about ⅓ of a
>   medium onion)
> ½ cup canned chickpeas, drained and rinsed
> ¼ cup grated raw beets
> ⅓ cup sprouts
> ⅓ cup raisins
> ¼ cup sunflower seeds
> Salt and pepper to taste
> ½ cup favorite salad dressing

1. Wash and drain lettuce leaves. If you have a salad spinner, spin the leaves dry.

2. Place romaine in a large salad bowl and layer all the other vegetables on top. Sprinkle sprouts, raisins, and sunflower seeds on salad. Toss with dressing or serve dressing in separate bowl on the side. Makes 2 meal-sized salads or 4 side salads.

Variation: If you like plain, uncooked tofu, add ½ **cup or more tofu cubes** to the salad.

Beets in a Salad?

They add color and crunch! Use the raw kind, not the pickled ones. Just peel them and grate them in, or cut into very small pieces. Beet bonus: When you buy fresh beets, save the greens to chop into a stir-fry. By the way . . . let's see, how should we put this . . . beets come out of you the same color they go in. So don't be alarmed.

Mama Stephie's Crunchy Chopped Salad

A salad doesn't require lettuce. This chopped salad is something interesting to add to a family meal or take to a summer picnic.

Dressing:

Juice from 2 lemons

¼ cup olive oil

½ cup chopped fresh cilantro (try to remove as many of the stems as possible)

½ cup fresh parsley, chopped

2 scallions, sliced

¼ to ½ teaspoon black pepper

2 or 3 cloves garlic, peeled, pressed, or finely chopped

Salt and pepper to taste

Salad:

2 carrots, chopped into small bite-sized pieces

2 celery stalks, chopped

2 tomatoes, chopped into small chunks

1 green pepper, seeds and inside ribs removed, chopped

1 small cucumber, peeled and chopped

15 ounce can artichoke hearts, drained and cut into bite-sized pieces (canned hearts of palm are another good "exotic" ingredient that you might want to try)

1 cup cooked or canned white beans, drained (and you don't have to chop these)

Any other crunchy vegetables you want to chop

1. Combine dressing ingredients in a bowl or a small bottle. Stir vigorously or shake well and set aside for 15 minutes to allow flavors to combine.

2. Meanwhile, chop vegetables and combine them with beans in a large bowl.

3. When dressing is ready, stir or shake again and add it to chopped stuff. Toss salad together and let the entire mixture sit for about 15 minutes. Makes 6 to 8 servings. Leftovers are good in a pita pocket for lunch.

insanely**easy**

Lemony Cukes
These light and fresh cucumbers go really well with Thai Coconut Curry (page 84) and other spicy, ethnic dishes.

> 1 cucumber, peeled and chopped into small
>   (½ inch to 1 inch) chunks
> ½ Tablespoon vegetable oil
> Juice from ½ lemon
> Salt and pepper to taste

1. Combine all ingredients in a bowl. Adjust seasonings to taste. Serves 4.

1-2-3 Steps to a Better Salad

1. *Go for the green. Lettuces with darker, greener leaves are generally more nutritious and taste better than iceberg lettuce. Try romaine, red leaf lettuce, mesclun, or other specialty salad mixes.*

2. *Add whatever you like: corn kernels, chopped green pepper, red onion, carrots, cauliflower, broccoli. Add crumbled tofu, canned beans, sunflower seeds, raisins, croutons, you name it. Think flavor. Think texture. Think crunch.*

3. *Remember that the smallest things can make a salad more interesting. "I like to change the consistency by cutting things differently, like grating carrots instead of chopping them, or vice versa," says Tovah, 17.*

Sesame Slaw

Coleslaw with an Asian twist. Delicious with sandwiches, veggie burgers, soy hot dogs, and curried dishes such as Thai Coconut Curry (page 84).

3½ cups prepackaged
    coleslaw mix
1 Tablespoon vegetable
    oil
1 Tablespoon sesame oil
1 to 1½ Tablespoons apple cider vinegar
⅛ teaspoon tamari or soy sauce (optional)
Salt and pepper to taste
2 teaspoons sesame seeds

1. Place coleslaw mixture in a bowl.
2. In a separate bowl, mix together remaining ingredients except for sesame seeds. Pour over slaw and toss to combine. Sprinkle with sesame seeds. Serves 4.

Christie's Creative Pasta Salad

Christie, 18, points out that her pasta salad is never the same twice. This recipe makes a big bowlful of salad—great to take to a party.

1 pound pasta (rotini are good, because the
    spirals hold lots of dressing)
1 green bell pepper, finely chopped
1 red or yellow bell pepper, finely chopped
4 to 6 pepperoncini (a mild, pickled pepper
    available at supermarkets), chopped
½ cup cubes of your favorite soy cheese or
    dairy cheese
¼ cup sliced black or green olives (remove
    pits first)

15 ounce can artichoke hearts, drained and
   quartered
2 scallions, finely sliced
¾ to 1 cup of your favorite dressing
1 large tomato, chopped
1 Tablespoon fresh chopped basil (or
   1 teaspoon dried basil, but fresh tastes
   much better)
Salt and pepper to taste
Soy or dairy parmesan cheese to taste
   (optional)

1. Cook pasta according to package directions or directions on page 90.

2. Meanwhile, combine all of the chopped veggies, except for tomatoes, in a bowl.

3. When pasta is done, drain and add veggie mix and dressing, tomatoes, basil, salt and pepper, and other seasonings, and mix. Chill before eating. Serves 8 or more.

Variation: Add any other favorite vegetables. Some good choices are **steamed chopped zucchini, steamed asparagus pieces,** or **finely chopped or sliced red onion.**

Try Organic, Locally Grown Produce

Some teens try to use organic vegetables (grown without chemical pesticides or fertilizers) in salads and in cooking. "My family belongs to an organic food co-op where the food comes right from the farm," says Rhea, 17. "It's nice to know where the food comes from." Some teens shop at their local farmers markets. Sixteen-year-old Patrick likes to buy locally grown food. "It takes a lot of transportation and energy to ship food from far away, and you never know what pesticides were used," he says. He plans his menu around what's available. "Whatever they happen to have at the market, I turn into a salad." Many people say organic and locally grown food tastes better, too.

Simple Basil Pasta Salad

Fresh basil makes this pasta salad special.

8 ounces radiatore, bowtie, or wagon-wheel pasta

1 medium-sized tomato, chopped into small chunks

½ cup pitted and sliced black olives

¼ cup finely chopped fresh basil

3 cloves garlic, peeled and finely chopped

2 Tablespoons olive oil

2 Tablespoons lemon juice

2½ teaspoons red wine vinegar

Salt and pepper to taste

> ### Pasta Salads
>
> *These are easy to make, inexpensive, and filling. Pasta salads are meant to be freeform—and fast. Just take some cooked pasta, whatever vegetables you have on hand (use frozen veggies if you're in a big hurry), some dressing, and a special, interesting ingredient or two (like artichoke hearts, black olives, or sun-dried tomatoes). Voilà—a masterpiece! Pasta salad travels well, so it's great for lunchboxes.*

1. Cook pasta according to package directions or directions on page 90.

2. Meanwhile, combine tomato, olives, basil, and garlic in a bowl. In a separate bowl, combine olive oil, lemon juice, and red wine vinegar.

3. When pasta is finished cooking, drain it and add to the tomato mixture. Add dressing and toss everything together. Add salt and pepper to taste. Makes 4 servings.

Variation: Add ½ **cup small cubes of soy or dairy cheese.**

Potato Salad

Take this creamy, dairy-free potato salad to your next get-together, and watch it disappear. If you don't want to peel the potatoes, make sure you scrub them well before chopping.

4 red or yellow potatoes, peeled (optional) and cut into 1 to 1½ inch chunks (about 4 or 5 cups total)

1 cup chopped celery
1 small onion, finely chopped
½ green pepper, chopped
½ to 1 cup tofu mayonnaise (store-bought
    or homemade, page 28)
Salt and pepper to taste

Try Tabouli

Tabouli (pronounced tuh-BOO-lee*) is a deliciously seasoned Middle Eastern grain salad. To make it quickly, start with a boxed mix (available in supermarkets) and add finely chopped **tomatoes, cucumbers, green peppers,** and fresh **parsley.** Great for picnics.*

---

1. Place potato chunks into a large saucepan and cover with water. Bring to a boil, reduce heat, and cook for about 10 or 15 minutes, or until potatoes are tender. Meanwhile, chop the veggies. When potatoes are finished cooking, drain them in a colander and let cool until just slightly warm. (You can run a little cold water over them to cool them faster, but not too long or they'll get mushy.) Place potatoes into a bowl.

2. Add celery, onion, green pepper, tofu mayonnaise, and salt and pepper to taste. Chill for a few hours before serving. Makes 6 to 8 servings.

insanely**easy**

Freeform Fruit Salads

It's probably impossible to make a bad fruit salad. All you have to do is rinse, peel, and cut up a few different kinds of your favorite fruit and toss together in a big bowl. If you want, you can add a light dressing or a little lemon juice. Or, instead of mixing the fruits together, you could arrange them on a platter—this is a great idea for a party.

Here are some good combinations to try. Or make up your own and give it a name.

Tart and Crunchy Salad:
    2 peeled and sliced **kiwi** fruits; **1 orange,** peeled, sec-

tioned, and cut into chunks; **1 granny smith apple** and **1 red pear,** cored and chopped; **1 sliced banana**.

Mango Fandango: **1 or 2 mangoes,** peeled and cut into cubes or small chunks; **1 apple,** cored and chopped; 1 sliced **banana; ½ cup blueberries**.

Melonhead: **1 cup cantaloupe** cubes or balls (cut melon in half and scoop out seeds first); **1 cup honeydew** cubes or balls; **1 cup watermelon** chunks; **1 cup fresh pineapple** chunks; **1 cup sliced strawberries**.

> ### Fruit Salad Tips:
> ■ *Squeeze in a little lemon juice to keep apples and pears from turning brown.*
> ■ *For a creamy fruit salad, mix in some soy or dairy yogurt (add 2 cups to any of the suggested combinations).*
> ■ *Drizzle fruit salad with melted chocolate, or top with apricot or raspberry preserves mixed with soy or dairy yogurt.*
> ■ *For an easy dessert, serve any fruit combination with a scoop of chocolate or fruit-flavored sorbet.*

Just Peachy: **3 diced peaches; 2 diced plums; 1 cup sliced strawberries; 2** peeled and sliced **kiwi** fruits.

Boisterous Berries: **1 cup sliced strawberries; ½ cup blueberries; ½ cup raspberries; ½ cup cherries,** pitted and halved.

Freeform Grain Salads

Forget about following recipes. This "non-recipe" gives you a framework to invent your own masterpiece. Just select your favorite things from each column and go crazy!

Here are some hints: Think of themes. For an Asian salad, for instance, add snow peas, peanuts, ginger, and a sesame oil dressing. For an Indian salad, include basmati rice and curry powder in your recipe. Also, experiment with different textures. For example, chewy dried apricots or raisins make a nice contrast to couscous or other fluffy grains.

Freeform Grain Salads

Grain	Veggie	Fruit or Nut	Seasoning	Dressing
Select 1 (**3 cups cooked**)	*Select 2 or 3* (**¼ cup each**)	*Select 1 or 2*	*Select 1 or more*	*Select 1* (**¼ cup or more**)
■ Couscous ■ Brown Rice ■ Quinoa* ■ Rotini, bowtie, or radiatore pasta ■ Basmati rice** ■ Cooked barley ■ Bulgur wheat***	■ Finely chopped carrot ■ Finely chopped green bell pepper ■ Finely chopped red bell pepper ■ Fresh diced tomato ■ Frozen corn kernels, thawed ■ Frozen green peas, thawed ■ Sliced snow peas ■ Finely chopped broccoli ■ Finely chopped cauliflower	■ ¼ cup raisins ■ ¼ cup dried currants, cranberries, or apricots ■ ⅓ cup finely chopped apple ■ ⅓ cup chopped fresh orange pieces, peeled, or canned mandarin orange pieces ■ ¼ cup chopped almonds, walnuts, or peanuts ■ 3 Tablespoons pine nuts ■ 2 Tablespoons sesame seeds ■ 2 Tablespoons sunflower seeds ■ 1 Tablespoon poppy seeds	■ 2 Tablespoons chopped fresh basil ■ ½ to 1 teaspoon dried basil ■ 2 Tablespoons chopped fresh parsley ■ 2 Tablespoons chopped fresh cilantro ■ ¼ to ½ teaspoon cumin ■ ¼ teaspoon turmeric ■ ¼ to ½ teaspoon dried ginger ■ ½ to 1 teaspoon curry powder ■ 1 teaspoon vegetable seasoning blend ■ 2 to 3 Tablespoons chopped red onion or green onion	■ Italian dressing ■ Favorite creamy bottled dressing ■ Garlic/lemon/olive oil combination ■ Sesame oil/rice vinegar combination

* Quinoa is a small, nutritious grain with a fluffy texture and slightly nutty taste. You can find it at a natural foods store.

** Basmati (pronounced bah-ZMAH-tee) is a rice with a warm, nutty fragrance available in brown and white varieties in most supermarkets and in natural foods stores.

***Bulgur wheat is a quick-cooking, fluffy grain that is good in pilaf and grain salad.

How to Cook Grains

In most cases, 1 cup of dry grain will produce about 3 cups cooked.

Grain Type	Cooking Time

Use 1 cup grain to 2 cups water for:

Brown rice	*45 minutes to 1 hour*
Basmati rice (white)	*20 minutes*
Basmati rice (brown)	*40 to 45 minutes*
Buckwheat (kasha)	*15 minutes*
Bulgur wheat	*15 minutes sitting in boiled water, covered, heat off*
Quinoa (pronounced KEEN-wah)	*15 minutes*
Couscous (pronounced KOOS-koos)	*15 minutes sitting in boiled water, covered, heat off*

Use 1 cup grain to 2½ to 3 cups water for:

Amaranth	*25 minutes*
Barley (pearled)	*45 minutes to 1 hour*
Millet	*40 minutes*
Wild rice	*1 hour or more*

Grain Tips

- Rinse grains in a strainer before cooking.
- For a nutty flavor, toast grains in a dry or lightly oiled skillet before cooking.
- Boil water first, and slowly stir in grain. Reduce heat, cover, and simmer until water is absorbed. Don't stir until grain is done.
- For more flavorful grains, use vegetable broth in place of part of the cooking water.
- If grain is too chewy, add a little extra water, bring back to a boil, and simmer again.

Do-It-Yourself Dressings

It's fun to make your own dressings to go on green salads or pasta salads. Try these:

Garlic Vinaigrette:
"This tastes best if it sits for a while before you eat it," says Tovah, 17. Mix together: **6 Tablespoons olive oil, 2 Tablespoons balsamic vinegar, 2 or more cloves of minced garlic,** a little **fresh chopped oregano,** and **salt and pepper** to taste.

Sesame Soy Dressing:
Combine ¼ **cup tahini, 2 teaspoons soy sauce, 2 to 3 Tablespoons lemon juice, 2 to 4 Tablespoons water,** and a dash of something sweet, such as **apple juice concentrate, barley malt, honey,** or **sugar.** Great on pita sandwiches.

Poppy Seed Dressing:
Combine ¼ **cup canola or olive oil, 3 Tablespoons red wine vinegar, 2 to 3 Tablespoons Dijon mustard, 1 1/2 Tablespoons natural maple syrup or honey, 2 teaspoons poppy seeds,** and **salt and pepper** to taste. Delicious as a pasta salad dressing.

More Salad Ideas

Corn salad: *Cut fresh **corn** from the cob, add **chopped red onion, sun-dried tomatoes, olive oil, balsamic vinegar,** and seasonings.*

Bread salad: *Use crusty **bread** that's gone a little stale; cut into cubes and add fresh **tomato chunks, green pepper pieces, basil, olive oil** and **lemon juice** or **balsamic vinegar.***

Bean salad: *Invent a mix of **canned beans,** fresh veggies and your favorite dressing.*

SOUPS

"Soup . . . I think it's just about one of the greatest things in this crazy world." —**Rhea, 17**

"Soup . . . I think it's just about one of the greatest things in this crazy world," says Rhea, age 17.

Top Ten Reasons to Eat Soup

1. Soup is easy to make and requires only one pot.

2. Soup is random. You can put whatever you want in it. (In fact, it's a great way to use up veggies that are getting old in your freezer or fridge.)

3. Soups are a tasty way to sneak veggies and other nutritious foods into your diet.

4. Soup can be made to suit any taste: creamy soup, chunky soup, spicy soup, noodle soup, you name it.

5. Soup is transportable. Pack some in a thermos or a sealable plastic container and you're good to go. (And most soups taste best as leftovers, anyway.)

6. Soup lets you blend in. You can't really tell just by looking at soup whether it was made with chicken stock or veggie stock, so you won't stand out as the weird vegetarian.

7. Soup is flexible. You can make a soup more filling by adding things like beans, noodles, rice, or more veggies.

8. Soup warms you up in the winter. And cold soups, like gazpacho, cool you down in summer.

9. Soup is inexpensive.

10. Soup is fun to make!

Quick Creamy Broccoli Soup

There's no dairy in this easy soup. Feel free to add some chopped potato or cauliflower along with the broccoli; it will cook down and make the soup even creamier.

3 cups frozen chopped broccoli
    (or fresh broccoli florets)
1 onion, cut into quarters
1 or 2 whole garlic cloves, peeled
1½ to 2 cups vegetable broth or water
    (or combination of the two)
¼ teaspoon salt
1 cup soymilk
2 Tablespoons flour
½ to 1 teaspoon basil
½ teaspoon parsley
Dash of vinegar
Salt and pepper to taste

1. In a large pot, combine broccoli, onion, garlic, broth or water, and salt. Cover pot, bring to a boil, and then simmer for about 15 minutes, or until everything starts getting soft.

2. Use a ladle to transfer ⅔ of the soup into a blender. Blend the soup until smooth. Pour back into saucepan and turn on heat to medium setting.

3. In a small bowl, combine soymilk with flour and whisk together until smooth. Pour mixture into soup and stir. Add basil and parsley and stir until soup begins to thicken. Add vinegar and salt and pepper to taste. Serves 2 to 4.

Gingered Carrot Soup

The secret ingredient in this recipe is a parsnip—a sweet-tasting root vegetable that looks like a big, cream-colored carrot. If you don't have a parsnip, increase the amount of carrot by another cup.

2 Tablespoons vegetable or olive oil,
  dairy-free margarine, or butter
1 small onion, chopped
½ to 1 teaspoon ground ginger
2 cups carrots, chopped
1 medium potato, peeled and chopped
1 cup parsnip, peeled and chopped
4 cups water (or a combination of water and
  vegetable broth)
1½ teaspoons salt (less if you're using a flavorful vegetable broth)
1 cup soymilk, rice milk, or dairy milk
½ to 1 teaspoon brown sugar (or other
  sweetener, such as honey, maple syrup, or
  apple juice concentrate)
1 teaspoon dried basil

1. In a large saucepan or soup pot, heat oil.
Add onion and sauté for 2 minutes.

2. Add ginger, carrots, potato, parsnip, water
or broth, and salt. Bring to a boil, cover, and simmer for about
30 minutes or so, until vegetables are extremely tender (they
should almost fall apart when you press them with a spoon).

3. Reduce heat to very low. Take a potato masher and mash the
veggies a bit. (Your goal is to make the soup creamier but leave
enough chunks to keep it interesting.)

4. Add milk, sweetener, and basil, turn heat up to medium-low,
and simmer for a few more minutes. Serves 4 to 6.

Dumplings

*Dumplings are easy to make and fun to eat. They add a chunky,
chewy treat to vegetable soups and stews. Just mix together **1 cup of
flour**, **¼ cup water**, and **1 fake egg** (page 156) or real egg and drop
by the spoonful into a soup that still has about 10 to 15 minutes to
simmer.*

Lorraine's Vegetable Wonder Soup

This is my mom's recipe for a veggie-filled soup that fills you up, warms you up, and gives you the energy to face just about anything. Don't let the long list of ingredients fool you; it's mighty easy and mighty good. You can use whatever vegetables you have—this is one soup you'll probably never make the same way twice.

A little water or 2 Tablespoons olive oil
1 onion, chopped
3 cloves garlic, peeled and chopped
¼ to ½ cup uncooked barley
5 cups more water
4 or 5 carrots
2 to 3 stalks celery, including leaves
2 potatoes, peeled
½ cup fresh parsley (if using dried, use a
    Tablespoon or two)
2 or 3 cups combination of any
    of the following: rutabaga
    (rutabaga is
    a tasty, orange-colored root
    vegetable), turnips, leeks,
    sweet potato, mushrooms, canned or
    cooked beans, zucchini. (Cabbage and
    cauliflower are good, too, but don't add
    these until about 10 minutes before the
    end to prevent the soup from tasting
    bitter.)
½ cup frozen green peas and/or green beans
½ cup frozen corn
15 ounce can vegetable broth
15 ounce can diced tomatoes
1 or 2 bay leaves
1 to 2 teaspoons dried basil
1 teaspoon sage (optional)
Salt and pepper to taste

1. Put oil or an inch of water in a large pot. Add onion and garlic to the water or oil. Simmer or sauté for a few minutes, until onions and garlic soften.

2. Add barley and water. Then begin chopping and adding the rest of the vegetables. Add all ingredients, except salt and pepper. Cover and simmer the soup for about an hour. About halfway through, check the consistency and add a little extra water or vegetable broth if you'd like. (If you don't add more, the soup will be fairly thick.) When soup is finished, remove bay leaves, add salt and pepper, and serve. Serves 6.

> **"**When making soup, you can basically just dump spices in until you find something that tastes good. I never measure spices or anything. (Make sure to keep tasting as you add.)**"** —**Tex, 15**

Chiqui's Corn Chowder

This fast chowder is adapted from a recipe from the mother of vegetarian Andrea, 19. Andrea's mom, Chiqui, uses corn cut fresh from the cob, but frozen corn kernels also work really well. Serve in a bowl with pieces of whole wheat bread on the bottom.

3 to 4 cups fresh or frozen corn
2 cups water, vegetable broth, or
    combination of the two
1 Tablespoon margarine or vegetable oil
1 small onion, finely chopped
2 stalks celery, chopped
½ teaspoon salt
1 Tablespoon cornstarch or arrowroot
    powder (both are plant extracts that work
    as thickeners)
1 cup water, vegetable broth, or soymilk
1 to 2 teaspoons finely chopped
    fresh parsley or dried parsley
Salt and pepper to taste

1. Place corn in a large saucepan and cover with the water or broth. Cover and cook for 10 to 15 minutes, or until corn is very soft. (If you have a pressure cooker, you can use that to cook the corn; it makes the soup even creamier.)

2. In a skillet, heat margarine or oil. Add onion and celery and sauté for a couple of minutes or until onions are translucent.

3. When corn is finished cooking, place ⅔ corn and its cooking liquid in a blender, along with onion-celery mixture. Add salt and cornstarch and blend until smooth and creamy.

4. Return mixture to soup pot, add one cup water, broth, or soy milk, and simmer until mixture thickens. Add parsley and salt and pepper. Serve immediately. Serves 4 to 6.

How to Make Your Own Veggie Broth

*It's easy to make your own vegetable broth to use as a base for other soups and stews. (It's also tasty instead of chicken soup when you don't feel well. Just add some cooked rice or noodles.) To make it, simply take lots of veggies, roughly chop them, and put them in a pot: **carrots, celery, parsnips, potatoes, canned tomato, garlic, onion, mushrooms**, whatever. You can also do this with scraps of veggies that you save as you cook throughout the week—anything from corn cobs to the ends of green beans. Cover with about **8 cups of water**, bring to a boil, cover, and simmer for at least an hour. Pour the veggies and broth through a large strainer and press the vegetables that remain in the strainer to get all of the good flavor into the broth. Add **salt** and a little **pepper**. The broth is now ready to use in recipes. It'll keep for several days in the fridge or several months in the freezer. Note: Some veggies, such as bell pepper, cabbage, and cauliflower, can get bitter when they cook too long, so you may want to leave them out of your broth.*

---

insanely**easy**

Instant Miso Soup Bowl

For a quick and tasty light snack, make a bowl of miso soup. Miso (pronounced MEE-soh) is a concentrated, fermented soybean paste used in traditional Japanese cooking. It comes in a variety of styles, from mellow-tasting white miso to dark, rich-tasting red miso.

For one person:
  1 cup water
  2 Tablespoons mild white or yellow miso
Optional Ingredients:
  A few thin slices of scallion (about
    ½ scallion)
  A few ½ inch cubes of firm tofu
  1 mushroom, sliced

1. Boil water. Place miso in a heat-proof bowl. Pour in a little of the boiled water and mix together to dissolve miso into a paste. Add remaining boiled water and stir.
2. Add optional ingredients of your choice. Let soup sit for a minute or two, until all ingredients are heated by the broth.

For four people:
  4 cups water
  2 sliced scallions
  ½ cup cubed firm tofu
  ¼ cup sliced mushrooms
  ½ cup mild white or yellow miso

1. Combine water, scallions, tofu, and mushrooms in a saucepan. Bring to a boil and turn off heat.
2. Spoon miso into a heat-proof bowl. Add enough boiled water from the pot to dissolve the miso into a thick, pasty liquid. Add miso to soup pot, stir, and serve.

Note: Don't boil soup again after adding miso. Boiling kills the beneficial enzymes in miso and destroys some of its nutritional value.

Bill's Amazing Autumn Stew
The hefty dose of paprika gives this colorful, spicy soup its kick. Experiment by changing the spices, or by adding extra broth (for thinner soup) or more vegetables (for thicker soup). As my husband, Bill, likes to point out, "There are no rules in this soup."

3 Tablespoons olive oil
1 large onion, finely chopped
3 to 5 cloves garlic, finely chopped
1 sweet potato, peeled and
    chopped into ¾ inch cubes
1 cup butternut squash, peeled
    and cubed
2 Tablespoons paprika
2 teaspoons turmeric
1 bay leaf
1 teaspoon salt
1 teaspoon pepper
Pinch of cayenne pepper (optional)
1 large tomato, finely chopped
1 green, red, or yellow bell pepper, finely
    chopped.
2 cups vegetable broth or water (canned
    broth is fine)
15 ounce can chickpeas, with liquid
2 cups of any combination of your
    favorite frozen vegetables, such as
    corn, green beans, or sliced okra
    (especially nice)
1 cup frozen green peas

1. In a large pot, heat oil. Add onion and garlic and sauté for about 3 minutes.

2. Add sweet potato and squash (you could omit the squash and add more sweet potato, but the squash is so good). Stir and cook for 5 minutes.

3. Add spices. Stir and add tomato and bell pepper. Cook for 1 minute, stirring constantly. Add broth and simmer for about 5 minutes.

4. Add chickpeas and frozen vegetables. Simmer for about 15 to 20 minutes, or until all vegetables are tender and flavors are blended. Serve with crusty bread. Makes about 6 servings.

Mushroom Barley Mambo

Barley is a grain that's often used in soup. It thickens the soup and adds a great texture.

3 Tablespoons olive oil

1 large onion, chopped

2 cloves garlic, peeled but left whole

2 carrots, peeled and chopped

2 stalks celery, chopped

2 cups sliced white button or brown cremini mushrooms (the brown ones have a deeper flavor)

½ to ⅔ cup barley

8 cups water (or combination of water and vegetable broth)

2 bay leaves

1½ teaspoons or more salt (you won't need as much salt if you're using vegetable broth)

Black pepper to taste

1 to 2 Tablespoons dried parsley or fresh chopped parsley

Splash of apple cider vinegar

1. In a large pot, heat oil. Add onion, garlic, carrots, and celery and sauté for 2 or 3 minutes. Add mushrooms; sauté for 2 minutes more.

2. Add barley, water, and bay leaves; bring to a boil, reduce heat, cover, and simmer for 35 to 45 minutes, or until barley is tender and chewy. Remove bay leaves. Smash garlic cloves with a spoon and stir into soup.

3. Add salt, pepper, parsley, and vinegar; simmer for 10 minutes more. Add more salt and pepper to taste. Serves about 6.

> ### Go Online!
>
> *"I like to get vegetarian recipes from the Internet. Tonight, after I finished my homework, I found a pretty easy soup recipe. It was really good—made with potatoes and peas, water, celery, garlic, cinnamon, ginger, pepper, and red wine vinegar," says Erin, 16.*

Mighty Minestrone

Minestrone is an Italian tomato-based vegetable and bean soup. You can be really creative when you make it. Experiment with different kinds of veggies, pasta, and beans, or by adding more or less water to make it soupier or more stewlike. This soup is delicious with dumplings (see page 121).

3 Tablespoons olive oil
1 onion, chopped
2 cloves garlic, peeled but left whole
2 stalks celery, chopped
28 ounce can whole peeled tomatoes,
    with liquid
6 cups water or vegetable broth,
    or a combination
2 bay leaves
2 teaspoons basil
1 teaspoon oregano
2½ cups frozen vegetable medley
    (including things like corn, green beans,
    carrots, lima beans)
1 cup canned chick peas or white beans, or
    any of your favorite beans, drained and
    rinsed
½ potato, finely diced
⅓ cup uncooked pasta shells or elbow
    macaroni
1 teaspoon salt, or to taste
Dash of apple cider vinegar

1. In a large pot, heat oil. Add onion, garlic, and celery, and sauté for about 2 or 3 minutes.
2. Add tomatoes and crush with a large spoon or a potato masher. Add water or broth and spices and bring to a boil. Reduce heat, cover, and simmer for about 30 minutes.
3. Smash garlic cloves with a spoon and stir into soup. Add frozen vegetables, beans, potatoes, and pasta. Cook for 20 to 30

minutes more, or until everything is tender.

4. Add salt and vinegar; simmer for a few more minutes.
Serves 6 to 8.

Dal

Dal (pronounced "dahl") is a
thick, simple, lentil or split pea

> ### Spruce Up Your Soup
>
> *"My big tip for soup is that if it's not*
> *tasting good, add tomato sauce," says*
> *Tovah, 17. "No matter how it tasted*
> *before, that will make it taste good."*
> *You could also add canned tomato or*
> *vegetable juice. A dash of lemon juice or*
> *balsamic vinegar at the end of cooking*
> *can improve flavor, too.*

soup that is popular all over Nepal and India. This version was
inspired by Mark, a college student who recently spent a year
abroad in Kathmandu. Mark sometimes uses leftover dal as a tor-
tilla filling—sort of like a multicultural burrito. It's also delicious
over cooked rice. Dal is pretty thick; if you like a thinner soup, add
an extra cup of water.

1½ cups lentils or yellow split peas
3 cups water
2 Tablespoons vegetable or olive oil
1 onion, finely chopped
1 or 2 teaspoons fresh ginger, finely chopped
Pinch of any of the following spices: cumin,
    turmeric, curry powder, dried mustard,
    crushed red pepper flakes, black pepper
1 teaspoon or so salt
Splash of lemon juice or apple cider vinegar
    (optional)

1. In a pot, combine lentils or peas with water. Bring to a
boil, reduce heat, and simmer for 30 to 45 minutes (or as Mark
suggests, "until you can hardly recognize that they're lentils or
split peas").

2. Meanwhile, in a skillet, heat oil and add onion and ginger;
sauté for about 2 minutes. Stir in remaining spices.

3. When lentils or peas are finished cooking, add salt and
onion-spice mixture. Stir in lemon juice. Serves 4.

Fast Black Bean Soup

It's fun to make black bean soup from dried beans, but to do that you need to soak the beans for hours ahead of time and cook them for a fairly long time. Canned black beans make soup that's really fast, easy, and delicious.

4 Tablespoons olive or
    vegetable oil
1 onion, chopped
3 teaspoons finely
    chopped garlic
½ cup chopped green pepper
2 carrots, sliced or finely
    chopped
½ to 1 teaspoon finely chopped jalapeño
    peppers, or 1 Tablespoon canned mild
    green chilies
1 teaspoon cumin
15 ounce can black beans with liquid
2 cups canned vegetable broth or 1 cup broth
    and 1 cup water
2 teaspoons lemon juice
1 Tablespoon finely chopped fresh cilantro
    (optional, but recommended!)
Tofu sour cream (page 51) or regular
    sour cream for topping (optional)

1. In a large sauce pan, heat oil, add onion and sauté for 1 minute. Add garlic and sauté 1 minute more.

2. Add green pepper, carrots, and jalapeño peppers or canned chilies and sauté for 4 more minutes.

3. Add cumin, beans, broth and water and cook for 20 minutes or more, until vegetables are tender.

4. Add lemon juice and cilantro and cook for a minute more. Top with tofu sour cream or dairy sour cream, if desired, and serve with tortilla chips or crusty bread. Makes 2 to 4 servings.

Gazpacho

In the summertime, a bowl of cold gazpacho makes a light, re-freshing meal.

4 ripe tomatoes, cut into quarters
½ cucumber, peeled and cut into chunks
½ bell pepper, cut into quarters (remove
　seeds and inner ribs)
1 scallion, roughly chopped
½ small onion, roughly chopped
1 clove garlic, peeled
Dash of red wine vinegar
Dash of olive oil
1 Tablespoon lemon juice
3 fresh basil leaves, chopped (optional)
2 Tablespoons fresh parsley, chopped
2 Tablespoons fresh cilantro, chopped
Pinch of red pepper flakes (optional, for a
　spicy, authentic flavor)
Salt and pepper to taste

1. Combine all ingredients in a food processor or blender.
2. Blend well, pour into a bowl, and chill for a few hours to let flavors meld. Eat with a chunk of crusty bread. Serves 4 to 6.

insanely**easy**

Refreshing Melon Soup

Cold fruit soup is great on hot days. It can be a meal—or a dessert.

1 very ripe cantaloupe or honeydew melon,
　cut in half and seeds removed
⅓ cup apple or orange juice or
　juice from 1 lemon mixed
　with ¼ cup water
1 teaspoon fresh chopped mint
　leaves (optional)
½ cup soy or dairy yogurt (optional)

> **"**I like to cook because it's a nice thing to do when people are over. Also, people are sort of surprised when you like to cook, especially when you're young.**"**
> —**Joseph, 18**

1. Cut melon into smaller pieces, remove peel, and cut into chunks. Puree in a food processor or blender.

2. Add juice, mint, and yogurt and blend everything together until smooth. Add extra juice if you'd like the soup a little thinner. Chill and serve. Serves 4 to 6.

Variation: Try adding **fresh strawberries, blueberries,** or **raspberries** to the soup (before or after blending).

ON THE SIDE

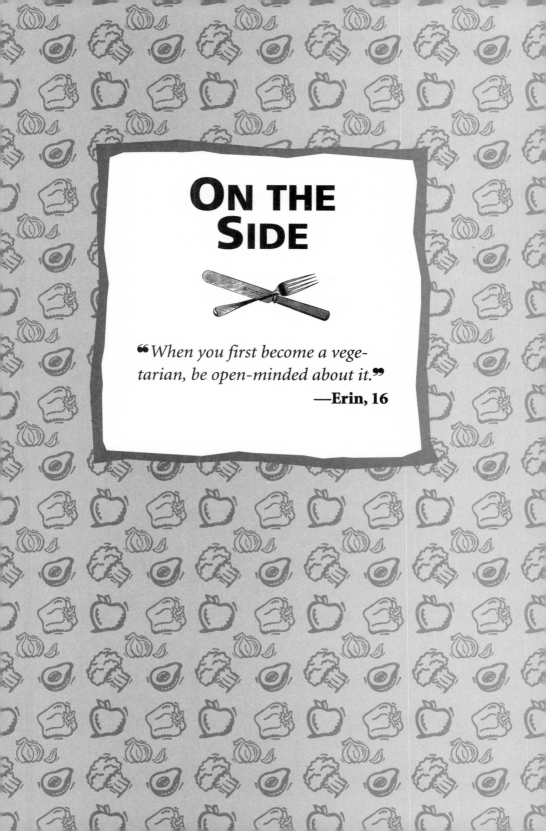

❝ *When you first become a vege-tarian, be open-minded about it.* ❞

—**Erin, 16**

Here are a few recipes for when you need a little something on the side. Some of these side dishes make great snacks, too. A few can be jazzed up to make a whole meal. (For example, you could serve the Sautéed Greens and Garlic over rice or noodles with some pasta sauce.)

Tangy Carrots

6 carrots, peeled and cut into 1-inch rounds
Water for steaming carrots
1 Tablespoon dairy-free margarine,
    butter, or vegetable or olive oil
1 teaspoon Dijon mustard
1 Tablespoon apple or orange juice
    concentrate
½ teaspoon cumin
Salt to taste

1. Steam carrots as instructed on page 137.
2. In a skillet, heat margarine, butter, or oil. Add mustard, juice concentrate, and cumin, stir together, and heat until bubbly.
3. Add carrots to mustard mixture and stir to coat all the pieces. Heat for 1 minute. Serves 4.
   Variations: Use half **carrots** and half **cauliflower florets.** Or add **2 Tablespoons chopped walnuts, slivered almonds,** or **golden raisins.**

Sautéed Greens and Garlic

Eat these greens with any meal, or make a sautéed greens sandwich. You'll need a big pot to fit all of these greens, but they cook down quite a bit. "Don't freak out the first time you cook fresh spinach and end up with only a cup. It shrinks!" notes Johanna, 19.

1 large bunch or 2 small bunches of dark
   leafy greens: choose from spinach, kale,
   collard, Swiss chard, beet greens, or a
   combination
1 to 2 Tablespoons olive oil
1 to 2 cloves garlic, finely chopped
1 teaspoon lemon or lime juice
Salt and pepper to taste

What's So Great About Greens?

Dark leafy greens are packed with vitamin C, beta-carotene, iron, fiber, and other nutrients that keep you healthy. Kale, collard, bok choy, and broccoli especially are packed with calcium—great for vegans!

1. Wash greens well to remove any dirt. (You can either fill the sink with water and swish the leaves around, or wash the leaves individually under running water.) Remove stems. Cut or tear greens into pieces —but not too small. Set aside.
2. In a skillet or large saucepan, heat olive oil and sauté garlic for 1 minute. Add greens and sauté for a few minutes, stirring occasionally, until leaves are wilted and bright green. Add lemon or lime juice and salt and pepper. Sauté for a minute more. Makes 4 servings.

Variation: For **Sesame Ginger Greens,** substitute **sesame oil** for half the olive oil when sautéing. Add **1 or 2 teaspoons tamari** and when the greens are finished, sprinkle with **sesame seeds.**

insanely**easy**

Broccoli with a Bite

1 medium bunch of broccoli
2½ Tablespoons vegetable or olive oil
3 or 4 cloves garlic, peeled and finely chopped
½ teaspoon turmeric (optional)
Salt, soy sauce, or tamari to taste

1. Wash and cut broccoli into bite-sized pieces to make about 2 ½ to 3 cups. Set aside.

Simple Steamed Vegetable Hints

■ *To steam vegetables:*

1. *Wash and chop into desired size and shape pieces: Trim ends off green beans and bottoms off asparagus; cut carrots into slices or matchsticks; cut broccoli and cauliflower into florets and chop the stems; remove tough stems from kale and other dark leafy greens and chop or tear into small pieces. To steam hard winter squash, cut open, remove seeds and skin, and carefully chop into pieces.*

2. *Fit a steamer basket into a medium-sized saucepan containing about ¾ inch of water.*

3. *Bring water to a boil, add vegetables, cover, and steam for 5 to 12 minutes, depending on veggie. Tender vegetables such as greens require just a few minutes. Tough root vegetables take longer.*

■ *Cook vegetables until tender but still crisp. Steamed vegetables are most delicious when they still have some crunch. Check the texture at various intervals by testing with a fork, or by tasting (cool it down under cold running water first).*

■ *Eat your vegetables plain or experiment with seasonings. A small touch of soy margarine or butter and salt is always nice. Or try a squeeze of lemon juice on your vegetables. Other ideas: Sprinkle vegetables with a little tamari, a drop of sesame oil, and a sprinkle of sesame seeds. Or try a dash of cumin, basil, dried ginger, or parsley.*

2. Heat oil in a large sauté pan, add garlic, and sauté for 1 to 2 minutes. Add turmeric, if using, and stir to coat the garlic. Add broccoli, stir, and sauté on medium heat for 1 or 2 minutes. Sprinkle salt, soy sauce, or tamari over broccoli, lower heat, cover, and cook for about 5 minutes, stirring once about halfway through. Remove cover, stir, and cook for about one minute more. Serves 2 to 4.

Peanutty Green Bean Stir-Fry

My friend Jennifer created this crunchy, colorful side dish.

3 cups fresh green beans
1½ teaspoons sesame oil

1½ teaspoons vegetable oil
1 to 2 cloves garlic, finely chopped
1 teaspoon finely chopped fresh ginger root
    or ½ teaspoon dried ginger
Pinch of cayenne pepper (optional, use it
    if you like spicy food)
½ cup chopped red pepper
Splash of tamari or soy sauce
Small handful of chopped peanuts
Black pepper to taste (optional)

> **"**When you first become a vegetarian, be open-minded about it. Lots of people say 'Oh, I couldn't do that. I hate vegetables.' That's because the way they're used to having them is in a little lump beside the roast beef. Try simple recipes for a little while, first. And don't overcook your vegetables.**"** —**Erin, 16**

1. Wash and trim green beans, then steam as directed on page 137, until bright green and tender but still crisp.

2. In a skillet, heat oils, add garlic and ginger, cayenne pepper (if using), and sauté for 1 minute. Add beans, red pepper, tamari or soy sauce, and peanuts, and stir-fry for a few more minutes, or until veggies are tender. Sprinkle with pepper and additional tamari or soy sauce, if desired. Serves 2 to 4.

Kim's Garden Blend

"I mostly learned how to cook through cookbooks and old family recipes, along with a little help from my mother," says Kim, 17. This is one of Kim's favorites. It's a fun way to use fresh corn in the summer.

4 ears fresh corn on the cob (or use 1½ cups
    frozen corn kernels)
½ small onion, chopped, or 2 scallions, finely
    chopped
½ green bell pepper, finely chopped

1 Tablespoon dairy-free margarine, butter, or
   olive oil
1 large tomato, chopped
Dash of salt
¼ teaspoon cumin
1 Tablespoon sugar or apple juice concentrate

1. Carefully cut corn from the cob. In a medium saucepan, mix together corn kernels, onion or scallions, green pepper, and margarine, butter, or oil. Cook over medium heat, stirring, for about 2 minutes. Lower heat, cover pan, and cook for 10 minutes.

❝I spent the first few years as a vegetarian eating lots of pizza and junk food and sweets. This not only made me fat, but I was not healthy! I have since started eating fruits, vegetables, whole grains, and beans. These are the staple foods to a healthy vegetarian diet.❞
—Kristy, 18

2. Add tomato and sugar or apple juice concentrate, stirring gently to blend. Cover and cook 5 minutes longer. Makes 4 or 5 side servings.

Roasted Rosemary Vegetables

This could be a side dish or, if you add some firm tofu (cut into cubes) or some cooked white beans, a main dish that you can serve with rice or thick pieces of bread. Leftovers are great for lunch.

6 cups combination of your favorite vegetables
   (Some vegetables to try include potatoes,
   carrots, green beans, red or white onion,
   celery, broccoli, cauliflower, cabbage,
   squash, asparagus, or zucchini. Beets are
   delicious roasted, but should be done
   separately; they'll turn other veggies red.)
5 cloves whole garlic, peeled
3 Tablespoons olive oil
1 Tablespoon fresh or dried rosemary
Salt and pepper

1. Preheat oven to 450° F. Combine vegetables, oil, and seasonings in a large baking pan, making sure that all vegetables are coated.

2. Bake uncovered for about 35 to 45 minutes, mixing once or twice during baking, until potatoes and other vegetables are tender (test with a fork). Makes about 4 servings.

Variation: Try other seasonings besides rosemary, such as **oregano, thyme,** and **sage.**

insanely**easy**

Baked Squash

Squash is sweet and delicious and loaded with nutrients. It's good topped with a tiny bit of soy margarine or butter and salt, or simply sprinkled with a little tamari or soy sauce. You can mash it up and use it in other recipes, such as Squashadillas (page 44).

> 1 small butternut squash, acorn squash, or
> delicata squash

1. Heat oven to 350° F. Cut open squash, scoop out seeds, and place cut side down on a lightly oiled pan or baking dish.

2. Bake for about 40 to 50 minutes, or until squash is tender (test with a fork).

To cook squash in a microwave: Cut squash in half and scoop out seeds. Place in microwave oven cut side up, and cover with waxed paper. (You could also put it in a covered microwave-proof baking dish.) Cook on high until squash is tender. Acorn and delicata squash take about 10 minutes. Butternut squash takes 10 to 14 minutes. Cooking times will vary, depending on oven wattage.

Note: **Acorn squash** is a small, dark green squash, shaped

Seasoned Spread for Bread or Vegetables

Take a couple of tablespoons of soft margarine or butter and add a pinch of your favorite herbs or spices, like fresh or dried basil, rosemary, oregano, fresh crushed garlic, or garlic powder. Spread some on bread or add a little to steamed vegetables for a surprise of flavor and color!

like an acorn, with ridges all the way around. **Butternut squash** is a beige squash with a bulb-shaped end. **Delicata squash** is a small, oblong, pale yellow squash with dark green and orange markings. Butter-

> ❝With cooking, I sometimes get frustrated when things don't turn out. But after about a week of peanut butter sandwiches and frozen macaroni and cheese, I'm usually back to cooking again.❞
>
> **—Kim, 17**

nut and delicata tend to be a little sweeter than acorn.

Variation: For an easy dessert, dot baked squash with **margarine** and **brown sugar** and pop it back in the oven for about 10 minutes.

Bonus: Don't throw away the **squash seeds;** you can bake them to make a tasty snack. Rinse the squash fibers from the seeds, spread seeds on a baking pan, and bake at 350° F for 30 minutes or so, until seeds are crisp toasted. Sprinkle baked seeds with **salt** or **tamari.**

insanely**easy**

Sharon's Applesauce (or Pear Sauce)

Applesauce is fun to make and much tastier than the prepared kind. You can eat it plain as a side dish or snack, or use it to top pancakes or French toast.

> 3 or 4 apples or pears
> ⅓ cup water or apple juice
> 1 cinnamon stick or dash of ground
>   cinnamon
> 1 teaspoon to 1 Tablespoon sugar, apple juice
>   concentrate, or natural maple syrup
>   (optional)

1. Peel apples or pears and cut them into chunks. Place fruit in a medium saucepan with water or apple juice and cinnamon.

2. Cook over medium heat until fruit is soft and has cooked down. Add sugar or other sweetener, if desired. Serves 4.

Garlic Mashed Potatoes

You may never make regular mashed potatoes again after tasting these.

> 6 cups water for cooking potatoes
> 5 or 6 medium-small potatoes, peeled and
>   cut into little chunks
> 3 to 4 cloves garlic, peeled
> 1 Tablespoon dairy-free margarine, butter, or
>   olive oil
> ¼ to ⅓ cup soymilk, rice milk, or dairy milk
> Salt and pepper to taste

1. Boil water in a large saucepan. Meanwhile, peel and cut potatoes.

2. Place potatoes and garlic cloves in boiling water and cook for about 12 to15 minutes or until potatoes are very soft. Turn off the stove. Drain potatoes and garlic in a colander and return to pan.

3. Add milk and mash with a potato masher. Add salt and pepper to taste and mix together. Makes 4 servings.

Potatoes and Greens

This is a good way to sneak some greens—and nutrients—into your diet. If you have leftovers, use it as a filling in Potato Puffs (page 46).

> 3 to 4 large potatoes, peeled and cut into
>   chunks
> 2 Tablespoons dairy-free margarine, butter,
>   or olive oil
> 1 cup sliced leek or ½ cup
>   chopped onion
> 3 cups kale, washed, stems
>   removed and chopped. (You
>   could substitute frozen
>   spinach or collard greens, but
>   if you've never had kale, give it a try!)

½ cup soymilk, rice milk,
  or dairy milk
½ cup vegetable broth
Salt and pepper to taste
Additional 1 Tablespoon
  dairy-free margarine,
  butter, or oil (optional)

> "Cooking is a lot of fun, and it's a way to connect with other vegetarians. If you meet someone else who's a vegetarian, you're going to end up talking about cooking and what kinds of tricks you have to make things work out."
>
> —**Rhea, 17**

1. Place potatoes in a large saucepan and add enough water to cover. Bring to a boil, reduce heat, and cook for about 10 to 15 minutes, or until potatoes are tender.

2. Meanwhile, in a large frying pan, melt margarine or butter, or heat oil, and add leek or onion and sauté for a minute or so. Add chopped kale or other greens and sauté, stirring often, for about 4 minutes, or until kale is deep green and wilted. Remove pan from heat and set on a cool burner until the potatoes are finished.

3. When potatoes are soft, use a colander to drain water. Turn off stove and place potatoes back in cooking pot. Add soymilk or milk, vegetable broth, salt, and pepper. Add kale mixture, extra margarine, butter, or oil, if using, and more salt and pepper to taste. Serves 4.

Sweet Potato Un-fries

4 sweet potatoes
4 Tablespoons vegetable oil
Salt

1. Preheat oven to broiler setting. Cut each potato in half, then into French-fry shaped strips or wedges along the length of the potato.

2. Put the fries onto a small-to-medium-sized baking sheet that will fit into the broiler portion of the oven. Drizzle potatoes with oil and mix with your hands to coat all the pieces. Put the pan under the broiler for about 10 minutes, turning once or twice, until fries are lightly browned.

> **"**I became vegetarian largely for health reasons, but it's made me much more compassionate toward animals.**"**
> —**Rhea, 17**

3. Change oven setting to 400° F, remove un-fries from broiler portion of the oven, place in regular oven, and bake for about 15 to 20 minutes. When fries are done, lift them onto a paper towel–lined plate, sprinkle with salt, and serve. Serves 4.

Variation: For **Sesame Un-fries**, use **white baking potatoes,** add **2 Tablespoons Sesame Seasoned Salt** (page 107) along with the oil before broiling/baking (toss with hands to coat).

Zucchini Sticks
These are delicious served with a creamy tofu dip or dressing.

1 large or 2 medium zucchini
¼ cup soymilk, rice milk, or dairy milk
1 cup flour
¼ cup cornmeal
½ to ¾ teaspoon salt
1 teaspoon onion powder
¼ teaspoon black pepper
3 Tablespoons vegetable oil

1. Peel and cut zucchini into French-fry shaped sticks.
2. Pour milk into a little bowl. In a separate bowl, combine flour, cornmeal, onion powder, and pepper.
3. Dip zucchini sticks into milk and then into flour mixture. Coat the sticks completely with the mixture.
4. Heat oil in a skillet until very hot. Carefully so as not to splatter the oil, use a spatula to place zucchini sticks into the oil. Fry for a few minutes on one side, then turn and fry on remaining sides. Turn frequently to check browning. Fries are finished when they are golden brown on all sides, about 5 minutes total. Remove with a spatula and place on a plate lined with a paper

towel to drain some of the oil. Sprinkle with additional salt, if desired. Serves 6.

Variation: For **Seasoned Zucchini Sticks,** add a teaspoon of any **spicy seasoning mix** to the flour mixture.

---

10 Ways to Love Vegetables

You announced that you're a vegetarian and your parents started laughing, because you hate vegetables. Here are some ways to get vegetables into your diet:

1. *Scoop them into a dip. Try Onion Spinach Dip (page 45), Hummus (page 29), or Baba Ghanouj (page 29).*

2. *Drink them. Try vegetable juice, tomato juice, or carrot juice. Hide vegetable juice in fruit juice (like carrot juice mixed with apple juice).*

3. *Hide them. Puree vegetables with a blender or food processor and add them to your favorite pasta sauce, lasagna, casseroles, or soups. Add cooked squash to pancakes or muffins. Out of sight, out of mind.*

4. *Try a new variety, like purple peppers instead of green ones. Supermarkets have lots of unusual varieties of vegetables. Be daring.*

5. *Combine them. Plain greens may sound boring, but try adding them to a stir-fry with other ingredients and seasonings.*

6. *Cut them into cool shapes. Cut carrots into very thin match-sticks; cut green peppers into rings.*

7. *Sauce them. For an easy corn sauce, just cook sweet corn then puree it by putting it through a strainer, and voila: corn sauce that is great over veggies and grains.*

8. *Freeze them. Munch on frozen veggies while still frozen—right out of the bag—as a snack.*

9. *Try them in a new recipe. Maybe it wasn't the vegetable you didn't like; maybe it was the way it was cooked and seasoned.*

10. *Remember, if at first it tasted gross, try, try again. You probably don't listen to the same music you did a year ago, or wear the same clothes, so you may not like or dislike the same foods.*

Tips provided by Carol Coughlin, R.D.

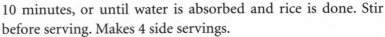

insanely**easy**

Speedy Spanish Rice

Here's an easy side dish to go with a burrito or tostada dinner.

1¾ cups water
1½ cups instant brown rice (available in
    supermarkets)
1 cup salsa

1. Boil water in a large saucepan.
2. Add brown rice and salsa. Reduce heat
to medium low and let rice cook for about
10 minutes, or until water is absorbed and rice is done. Stir
before serving. Makes 4 side servings.

insanely**easy**

Great Garlic Bread

*Real garlic cloves give this garlic bread real attitude. Great with a
pasta dinner.*

4 Tablespoons olive oil, dairy-
    free margarine, or butter
4 or more fresh cloves garlic,
    peeled and very finely
    chopped
½ to 1 whole loaf Italian bread, unsliced
    or sliced

1. In a small bowl, mix together oil, margarine, or butter and
garlic.
2. If bread is unsliced, use a serrated knife to slice bread
without cutting all the way through the bottom of the loaf.
(That way people can tear off their own slices as the bread is
passed around the table.) Spread the garlic mixture on each
bread slice.
3. Wrap in foil, leaving top open, and bake for 10 minutes.
Serves 6 to 8.

What's New on Your Menu?

It's fun to choose a new or exotic ingredient and experiment with it in your cooking. "One of my new things is coconut milk," says Patrick, 16. "It tastes really, really good." He made up his own recipe for coconut veggies. "Take potatoes, carrots, squash, or anything you want, and cut them up into small pieces. Then cook them in 2 parts water to 1 part coconut milk, adding the potatoes and carrots first, because they take longer to cook. Just boil the vegetables right in there—but don't overcook them, or the coconut milk gets oily."

Experiment with seasonings such as soy sauce or tamari, basil, curry powder, and ginger. "I just found a new herb at the store; it's called lemongrass," Patrick says. Lemongrass is a long, tough stalk with a light lemon fragrance and taste. You have to pound the stalk open to get to the tender, flavorful center.

Cornbread

Cornbread is the perfect side for soup, chili, or stew.

1 cup cornmeal
1 cup flour
½ teaspoon salt
2 Tablespoons sugar (see note)
1 teaspoon baking powder
½ teaspoon baking soda
1¼ cups soymilk, rice milk, or dairy milk
5 Tablespoons vegetable or olive oil
1 teaspoon apple cider vinegar

1. Preheat oven to 350° F. In a large bowl, combine cornmeal, flour, salt, sugar, baking powder, and baking soda.
2. In a small bowl or measuring cup, mix together milk, oil, and vinegar.
3. Add milk-oil mixture to dry ingredients. Blend together just until moist, but not longer.
4. Oil a small square baking pan (or, if your family has one, a cast

> " The best approach to vegetarianism is variety! It's important to have lots of recipes and a support system—whether through email lists on the Internet or from veggie friends who live in the area. "
> —**Andrea, 19**

iron skillet), and bake for 20 to 25 minutes, or until toothpick inserted into the center comes out clean. Remove from oven, cool, and cut into pieces.

Note: You may substitute **2 Tablespoons honey, barley malt, maple syrup,** or **apple juice concentrate** for the sugar. Add it to the liquid ingredients and reduce milk to 1 cup.

Variations:

Cornbread Muffins: Pour batter into oiled muffin tins and bake for 15 to 20 minutes, or until muffins are golden brown and firm.

Mexican Cornbread: Add ¾ **cup frozen corn kernels,** ¼ **cup canned diced green chilies** (drained), and **2 sliced scallions** to batter before baking.

Cornbread Fritters: Add ¾ **cup frozen corn kernels** and ¼ **cup canned diced green chilies** (drained) to batter. In a skillet, heat about ½ **inch oil** until very hot. Drop spoonfuls of batter into the oil and fry until golden brown on both sides, turning fritters occasionally during frying. Delicious for breakfast!

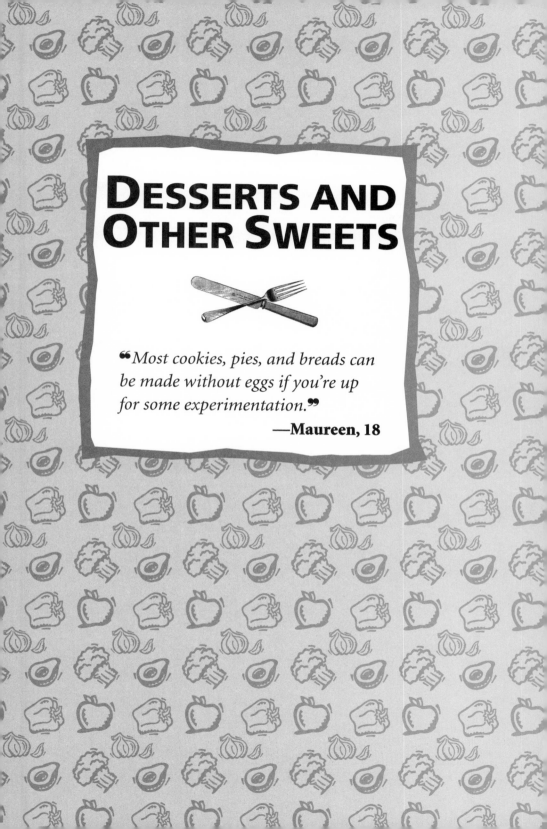

DESSERTS AND OTHER SWEETS

“ *Most cookies, pies, and breads can be made without eggs if you're up for some experimentation.* ”

—Maureen, 18

Some people are surprised to learn that vegetarians like to eat desserts and sweets just like everybody else. Here's an assortment of tasty treats.

Chocolate Coma

With two ingredients, this little piece of chocolate heaven couldn't be easier to make. Just be sure to allow time to chill for at least 4 hours. (Thanks to Karin for the inspiration.)

12 ounce package soft, firm, or extra-firm silken tofu (see note)

12 ounce package semi-sweet chocolate chips (some brands contain milk products; read labels if you are vegan) or sweetened or unsweetened carob chips

1. Puree tofu in a blender or food processor.

2. In a small saucepan, melt chocolate or carob chips over low heat.

3. Add melted chocolate or carob to tofu and blend until smooth. Pour into dessert dishes and chill for at least 4 hours.

> ### Graham Cracker Crust
> *To make your own graham cracker crust, grind **12 graham crackers** in a food processor or blender to make crumbs. Add **5 Tablespoons soft soy or dairy-free margarine** and process until well blended. Press mixture into a pie pan.*

Note: Soft silken tofu will produce a more pudding-like consistency. Firm or extra-firm tofu will make a firmer dessert.

Variations:

Chocolate Coma Pie: Pour into a **ready-made graham cracker pie crust** (or see instructions for making your own) and chill at least 4 hours.

Chocolate Raspberry Coma Pie: Add **8 to 10 ounces raspberry all-fruit preserves** to chocolate-tofu mixture and blend. Pour into crust and chill.

Chocolate Coma Freeze: Spoon mixture into a freezer-safe container and freeze until firm. Spoon into dessert dishes to serve.

Easiest Ever Berry Crisp

Using store-bought granola as a topping makes this dessert a snap. Serve it warm with vegan or dairy ice cream.

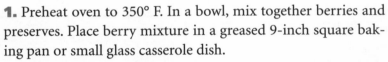

2½ cups fresh or frozen berries such as blueberries, raspberries, blackberries, or sliced strawberries (you can use all one kind or mix them up)
½ cup apricot preserves (the fruit-only kind works best)
1½ cups of your favorite granola
A little dairy-free margarine or butter

1. Preheat oven to 350° F. In a bowl, mix together berries and preserves. Place berry mixture in a greased 9-inch square baking pan or small glass casserole dish.

2. Spread granola evenly on top of the berries, and scatter little dots of margarine on top of the granola.

3. Bake for about 25 minutes, or until granola looks a little browned and berries look juicy and bubbly. Serves 4 to 6.

Apple-Date Dessert

You won't believe that there's no sugar in this very sweet dessert! Using dates as a sweetener is an ancient concept. You can serve this dessert in little bowls, or pour the mixture into a ready-made pie crust and bake according to crust instructions.

10 ounces dates, pitted
1 cup water

1 Tablespoon lemon juice
6 medium apples, peeled, cored, and thinly
    sliced
1 teaspoon cinnamon

1. In a saucepan, cook dates in ½ cup water for 10 minutes.
2. Add remaining water, lemon juice, apples, and cinnamon.
Mix together, cover, and simmer until apples are soft but not
mushy, about 5 to 10 minutes. Serves 6.

Laura's Vegan Chocolate Chip Cookies
*My friend Laura is the queen of vegan baking. She always has
some new dairyless recipe up her sleeve. Your friends will gobble
these up.*

1 cup dairy-free margarine
¾ cup sugar
¾ cup brown sugar
¾ to 1 teaspoon salt
2 homemade fake eggs (see page 157)
1 Tablespoon vanilla
2½ cups flour (actually, you can use up to 4
    cups of flour—the more flour you use, the
    denser, chewier the cookie; the amount list-
    ed here is for a texture that most people like)
1 cup nondairy semi-sweet chocolate chips.

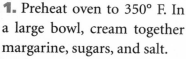

1. Preheat oven to 350° F. In
a large bowl, cream together
margarine, sugars, and salt.
2. In a small bowl, beat "eggs."
Then add to margarine-sugar
mixture. Add vanilla and
combine. Slowly, little by little,
add flour, stirring constantly
to combine. Continue until all
flour is well combined (it will

"If you're vegan, rice milk and soymilk
are great replacements for milk in
recipes (try the vanilla-flavored kind for
a delicious flavor). And most cookies,
pies, and breads can be made without
eggs if you're up for some experimentation," says Maureen, 18. (For tips, see
"Baking Without Eggs," page 156–57.)

get harder to combine the more flour you add).

3. Mix in chocolate chips. Form dough into 1-inch balls and place on an ungreased baking sheet. Then, as Laura puts it, "flatten them with a fork, wish them well, and put them in the oven." They'll be ready in about 10 to 12 minutes, or when golden brown. Makes about 3 dozen cookies.

Kim's Grandma's Ginger Cookies

"This recipe has been in my family for about four generations, and it's vegan, too," says Kim, 17.

1 cup molasses
1¼ cup sugar
1 Tablespoon baking soda
1 cup dairy-free margarine
1 cup hot water
1 teaspoon powdered ginger
1 teaspoon cinnamon
1 teaspoon ground cloves
3 cups flour
Powdered sugar for sprinkling

1. Preheat oven to 350° F. In a bowl, mix together molasses, sugar, baking soda, margarine, and water.

2. Add spices. Little by little, add flour and combine to form a stiff dough. If dough is too sticky, add a little more flour. If you have time, refrigerate the dough for a couple of hours before rolling it out; it will be easier to work with.

3. On a floured counter, roll the dough with a rolling pin and cut into shapes with cookie cutters. Place on an ungreased baking sheet and bake for 10 to 12 minutes. Top with powdered sugar or your favorite frosting. Makes about 3 dozen cookies.

Mango Freeze

This dessert goes well with spicy food. You could skip the freezing process altogether and pour the blended mixture into glasses to make smoothies.

8 ice cubes
2 to 3 mangoes, peeled and cut into chunks
¼ cup orange juice concentrate
1 cup soymilk, rice milk, or dairy milk

1. In a blender, crush ice cubes. Add mangoes, orange juice, and milk. Blend on high speed for a minute or two, until everything is smooth.

2. Pour into a shallow plastic container or bowl, cover, and place in freezer until frozen to the consistency of a soft ice cream, stirring occasionally during the freezing time. Serves about 4.

    Variation: For a tropical flavor, substitute ½ **cup canned coconut milk** for ½ cup of milk in recipe.

Baked Pears or Apples
with Spiced Orange Sauce

This is an easy but elegant dessert. The orange sauce bakes right inside the fruit.

4 pears or apples
2 Tablespoons raisins
2 Tablespoons walnuts, chopped
2 Tablespoons orange juice concentrate
2 Tablespoons water
2 Tablespoons maple syrup
¼ teaspoon cinnamon
¼ teaspoon cardamom

1. Preheat oven to 375° F. Wash fruit. Using a small knife, remove the cores from the fruits, but leave the base of the fruit intact. The fruits should be able stand up on their own; if they are wobbly, you can cut a slice from the bottom to create a base. Stand the fruits in a baking pan.

2. In a small bowl, combine raisins, walnuts, orange juice, water, maple syrup, cinnamon, and cardamom.

3. Spoon the mixture into the center of each pear or apple. Fill the pan with about an inch of water to prevent sticking and scorching. Bake about 30 minutes, or until fruit is tender when pierced with a fork. Let fruit cool for at least 15 minutes before serving. Serves 4.

Baking Without Eggs

Baking without eggs can be a little tricky, because eggs do several important things. For one thing, they provide leavening, *which means they make things rise. They also provide* binding, *which means they hold things together. They also add some* liquid. *So if you're leaving out the eggs, you have to find something else to do all of those things.*

In baking, there's definitely a chemistry going on between the liquid ingredients, the dry ingredients, and the leavening ingredients. In place of the eggs in your favorite recipes, try the following:

Applesauce: *Add about ¼ cup in place of an egg. This holds things together and adds moisture, but it doesn't do that much in the way of helping things rise. For that, you might need to add a little extra baking powder (about ½ teaspoon).*

Banana: *Use ½ banana, mashed, for one egg in sweet baked goods. (This is good only in things that will work with a banana taste.) Also add about ½ teaspoon extra baking soda.*

Tofu: *Use about ¼ cup mashed silken tofu for one egg. Also add ¼–½ teaspoon extra baking powder.*

Prune puree: *You can puree your own or purchase pureed prunes in the baking aisle of the supermarket. You can also use baby food prunes. Use about ¼ cup prunes plus ½ teaspoon extra baking powder. (Prunes will add sweetness to a recipe.)*

Baking powder: *Add an extra ½ teaspoon baking powder and about 2 tablespoons extra liquid to replace one egg in a recipe.*

Powdered egg replacer: *This stuff is great. It's a powdered mix, available in natural foods stores, that you blend with water to replace an egg in recipes. It works really well. It seems pricey* *(about $4.50 or so a box), but a box lasts a really long time, so it's worth it.*

Flax seed: *Flax seeds are available at natural foods stores. This flax seed mixture can be used in place of 2 eggs: Grind **3 tablespoons flax seed** to a very fine powder in a blender. Add ½ **cup water** and blend until the mixture becomes thick, resembling raw egg whites. Fold it into cake batter at the end of mixing for light vegan cakes, but only use in recipes that call for 2 or 3 eggs at the most. (This recipe used with permission from* Good News About Good Food *by Carol M. Coughlin, R.D.)*

Homemade Fake Egg: *Use the following recipe in place of one egg in baked goods; it works really well in cookies. It's best to whip it up right before adding it to the recipe. (Note: This recipe is not meant to replace eggs in really eggy dishes, like scrambled eggs.)*

Fake Egg

1 teaspoon baking powder
½ teaspoon baking soda
2 Tablespoons flour
3 Tablespoons water

Combine ingredients in a small bowl and mix together with a fork or wire whisk until foamy.

Eggless baking can sometimes be a daring adventure, but that doesn't mean you shouldn't experiment. If you end up with hockey pucks instead of cookies, don't worry. Try something different next time.

Sweet Potato Pumpkin Pie

A special finish for a holiday meal, or anytime in the fall or winter. This pie is best when made one day ahead and stored in the refrigerator overnight to firm.

1 large sweet potato
15 ounce can pumpkin
½ cup brown sugar, natural maple syrup, or

honey (the pie will be softer if you use a
liquid sweetener)
1 cup soymilk, rice milk, or dairy milk
3 Tablespoons vegetable oil
1 teaspoon cinnamon
½ teaspoon nutmeg
½ teaspoon ginger
2 teaspoons vanilla
3½ Tablespoons cornstarch dissolved in 2 to
3 Tablespoons water
Ready-made graham cracker pie crust (or
use crust recipe on page 151)

1. Pierce sweet potato several times with a fork and bake in the microwave for about 10 minutes on high setting or about 35 minutes in a 400° F oven.

2. When potato is cool, scoop potato flesh from skin, place in a bowl, and mash with a potato masher until smooth. Add pumpkin and sweetener; place in a blender and blend until smooth.

3. Heat oven to 425° F. In a separate bowl, combine soymilk and oil; add to sweet potato-pumpkin mixture.

4. Add spices, vanilla, and dissolved cornstarch; stir until well blended. Pour mixture into the crust. Bake for 15 minutes at 425° F; then reduce heat to 350° F and bake for 40 to 50 more minutes. To prevent crust from getting too brown, create a shield with aluminum foil around the crust part before placing in the oven; remove the foil when there is about 25 minutes left to the baking time. The pie is done when the center is firm and set. Remove from oven and cool. Serves 8.

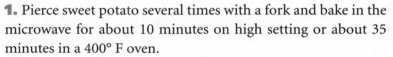
insanely**easy**

Peanut Crispy Bars

These crispy treats require no baking. They're great to pack in a lunch.

3 cups crispy brown rice cereal (available in a
natural foods store)

½ cup peanut butter

½ cup honey, natural maple syrup, or barley
malt (each of the sweeteners has a unique
flavor, so experiment to discover your
favorite)

1 teaspoon vanilla

½ teaspoon cinnamon (optional)

⅓ cup mini or regular sized semi-sweet
chocolate chips (optional)

1. Pour cereal into a large bowl and set aside.

2. In a small saucepan, heat peanut butter
and sweetener until softened.

3. Stir in vanilla and cinnamon (if using).
Remove from heat and pour into cereal (it will be very
sticky; use a spatula).

4. Stir to combine, and add chocolate chips (if using); stir
again to combine. Press into an oiled 9-inch square baking pan
and set a small sheet of plastic wrap or wax paper on the top;
use the wrap or paper to keep your hands clean as you press the
mixture solidly into the pan. Refrigerate for an hour or so
before cutting.

Which Sweetener to Use?

*Some vegans don't use honey because it comes from an animal.
You can use maple syrup, rice syrup, or barley malt instead. In
some recipes, apple juice concentrate works very well. If you are
using a liquid sweetener in a recipe that calls for regular sugar,
decrease the liquid in the recipe by ¼ cup for every cup of sweetener
used.*

*Some vegans avoid white sugar, because some white sugar may
be whitened using charred animal bones. Instead, you can use date
sugar, available at natural foods stores. (Some white sugars are
cruelty-free; for information, contact the Vegetarian Resource
Group for information: Vegetarian Resource Group, P.O. Box
1463, Baltimore, MD 21203; www.vrg.org.)*

Becca's Chocolate Nutty Truffles

This quick, no-bake truffle will satisfy every sweet tooth, and its rich, nutty center provides protein.

¼ cup sliced almonds
¼ cup cashews
1 cup favorite nut butter: almond,
    cashew, or peanut
4 Tablespoons maple syrup
¼ cup dates, chopped
¼ cup chocolate chips
⅛ cup powdered sugar
2 Tablespoons unsweetened cocoa
¼ teaspoon cinnamon

1. In a skillet containing no oil or liquid, combine the almonds and cashews. Heat over a low flame, stirring frequently, just until you start smelling a toasty, warm aroma. (Keep watching and don't let them burn.) You can also toast them for 2 minutes in a toaster oven set on a low setting.
2. In a bowl, mix together nut butter, maple syrup, and chocolate chips. Add nuts and stir to combine. Set aside.
3. In a small bowl, mix sugar, cocoa, and cinnamon.
4. Make teaspoon-size balls of the nut butter mixture and roll in the sugar-cocoa mixture until evenly coated. Place on wax paper and eat, or harden in refrigerator for 30 minutes. Makes 25 to 30 truffles.

    Variation: For **Lemony Nutty Truffles,** use **sesame butter** (oil poured off) or **cashew butter.** Leave out chocolate chips and cinnamon. Add ¼ **cup coconut flakes, 1 teaspoon finely chopped lemon zest** (the outermost rind of the lemon), and **1 Tablespoon lemon juice** to the nut butter mixture. Roll the truffles in **plain powdered sugar.**

COLLEGE CUISINE

" *With six hundred people living in a dorm, you'll definitely find other vegetarians.* **"**

—Joey, University of Illinois

When you head away from home and into the college dorm, what do you do for chow?

For starters, savor the independence! For the first time in your life, you get to eat the way you want, without having your parents eyeball everything that goes onto your plate. That sounds great, but how easy is it to find or prepare vegetarian food when you're stuck on a college meal plan or cooking out of a hot pot? Suddenly, you don't have your parents' refrigerator to raid.

Whether you eat in the school cafeteria, cook in your dorm room, or share an apartment or house with other students, you can eat well and have a good time as a vegetarian. This section is full of advice from teens who are doing just that.

Head to the Cafeteria

Lots of college students find that it's not so hard finding vegetarian food. "More and more colleges are offering vegan or at least vegetarian options, so don't assume you'll have problems being a vegetarian at school," says Tovah, a student at Smith College. According to *Restaurants and Institutions* magazine, many of the nation's colleges and universities are expanding the vegetarian selections in their cafeterias.

How much you find to eat will depend on your school and how strict a vegetarian you are. Some schools have vegan options on a regular basis, while at other schools, the vegetarian choices always have cheese. But there are ways to get by, says Tovah. "If your cafeteria doesn't have a vegan option at every meal, do they have a salad bar? A pasta bar? If they have both,

How to Veggie-fy Your Cafeteria

It's entirely possible to get more vegetarian foods served in your college dorm or camp dining hall, but you'll have to do some research, some negotiating—maybe even some public relations. Consider these suggestions from other students who have successfully changed their cafeteria menus:

Be organized: *Don't just complain about the food. Arrange a meeting with your food service directors and convince them that there is a need and market for healthy vegetarian food. Conduct a survey in your dorm, if possible, to find out if other students would eat a vegetarian or vegan entree.*

Be specific: *Explain exactly what you mean by vegetarian or vegan. (No chicken stock, no fish, no eggs, etc.)*

Be understanding: *There will be limits to what can be done, so don't be too pushy.*

Be helpful: *Supply recipe ideas, or arrange for a student taste test. Doing this kind of footwork will increase your chances of getting the meals you want.*

Be supportive of changes that are made: *Encourage other people in the dorm to try the new food. And definitely have all of your happy vegetarian friends write thank you notes to the food service director for a job well done!*

For institution-quantity recipes to share with your food service director, contact:

Vegetarian Resource Group, *P.O. Box 1463, Baltimore, MD 21203; www.vrg.org.*

Dietitians in College and University Food Service, *c/o Susan Davis Allen, M.S., R.D., 605 South Madison St., Lancaster, WI 53813.*

Physicians Committee for Responsible Medicine, *5100 Washington Ave., N.W., Suite 404, Washington, DC 20016; www.pcrm.org.*

you can be creative with pasta and tomato sauce. I add olives, garbanzo beans, sunflower seeds, pieces of tofu, and mushrooms from the salad bar to make a much more nutritious, tasty meal." Check out the salad bar at breakfast time, too: at some schools, you'll find a good assortment of fruit.

Even if you don't see anything you can eat in the cafeteria, you can try talking to the food service director to see if you can get some meatless options on the menu. "From my experience, if you talk with the people in the cafeteria, they'll work with you. You'll find that they're pretty reasonable people," says Joey, a student at the University of Illinois. Don't expect to get tofu lasagna on the menu overnight, he warns. "But if you ask them to provide some sort of basic grain, they'll usually do it."

The truth of the matter is, even if your school has some vegetarian food, you may still have to look for ways to keep your menu interesting. Mollie, a vegan student at Michigan State University, enjoys the tabouleh, rice, vegetables, and salad bar in her cafeteria. "But it gets pretty old after eight months or so," she says. If you're suffering from burnout, try keeping a good stash of vegetarian snacks and supplies in your dorm room to supplement the cafeteria fare. "You may want to try to get a reduced meal plan, and use the extra money to buy food at a local health food store," suggests Laura, a student at Iona College in New York.

Cooking for Yourself

Don't let the fact that you don't have a full kitchen limit you. There are lots of things you can make in your dorm room using a hot pot, toaster oven, or other appliances. (Make sure you check with your school's policy for cooking appliances; some schools don't allow certain things.) "I have a microwave, refrigerator, and toaster in my room, so it's very convenient," says Robyn, a student at Ball State University in Indiana. "When I'm in a hurry, usually at lunch, I make lots of prepackaged things. I'll just throw something in the microwave and I'm on my way. And for breakfast, I usually throw a bagel in the toaster or something." A dorm room refrigerator (you can rent one of these) will keep your food fresh.

You can do a lot with minimal appliances. "In my microwave, I like to make brown rice and baked potatoes," says Joey. You can also heat up frozen vegetarian Italian entrees that you buy from the supermarket, like spaghetti marinara. A toaster oven is great for toasting bagels and melting soy or dairy cheese over sandwiches. Make a Toasted PB and Banana sandwich: toast bread or bagel, spread it with peanut butter, spread it with honey or jam, and top with sliced banana. Pita pizzas are also easy to make with a little bottled spaghetti sauce, frozen veggies, and soy cheese or dairy cheese. For hotpot ideas, see page 167.

If your dorm has a shared cooking space, you have even more options. "My school has a kitchen in every dorm for students to prepare meals if they want—there is an oven, a stove, a microwave, a refrigerator, and a freezer," says Melanie, a student at Vassar College in New York. "I used that kitchen to make a nice vegan Thanksgiving dinner." Robyn uses her hall's kitchenette on a regular basis. "I make falafel, chili, things like that for dinner." Joey took his pressure cooker to school to use in his dorm's kitchen. It comes in handy for beans and other slow-cooking things.

The dorm can be a great place to meet other vegetarians and share experiences—and food. Look around, ask around. "With six hundred people living in a dorm, you'll definitely find other vegetarians," says Joey. And don't be afraid to welcome others into your little dorm room restaurant. "It really helps to explain to your roommates and other people what you're doing and why you're doing it."

It can get lonely eating alone in your dorm room, so try to share meals as much as you can. Or make it a group effort. "Sometimes my friends and I pick one person's room or dorm and cook Chinese food," says Robyn. Dinner is a time for good conversation as well as good food.

Hotpot Creations:

■ *Pasta, couscous, instant brown rice, or other fast cooking grains: Top them with pasta sauce, canned beans with salsa, or canned vegetarian chili. Make your own peanut sauce by mixing peanut butter, soy sauce, water, rice vinegar, and a dash of honey or other sweetener, and eat it with your pasta.*

■ *Racy Ramen: Cook some ramen noodles and dress them up with frozen green peas or other veggies, as well as your favorite spices. Look for vegetarian ramen noodle packets in a natural foods store. Most supermarket varieties are made with meat broth; check ingredients to find a vegetarian one.*

■ *Student's Stir-fry: "You can make an easy stir-fry with whatever vegetables you can find cheap at the supermarket, sautéed with onions and tomato sauce," says Tovah.*

■ *Potatoes with an Attitude: Make some instant mashed potatoes and sprinkle with garlic powder. Or, make your own garlic mashed potatoes using the recipe on page 142 (just cut the pota-toes into really small pieces so that they cook quickly).*

■ *Noodles in a Pot: Cook elbow noodles and mix with green peas or other veggies and cottage cheese. Sprinkle with veggie seasoning blends, such as Mrs. Dash. If you're a vegan, use pasta sauce instead of the cottage cheese, crumble in some extra-firm tofu, and add garlic powder.*

■ *Oatmeal or other hot cereal: Top with dried fruit, nuts, and yogurt*

■ *Tofu Veggies: Steam some frozen veggies and cubes of extra firm tofu. Drizzle with soy sauce. (You can make instant brown rice first and serve the veggies and tofu over it.)*

A Vegetarian Student's Pantry

You don't need all of these things, but this list will give you an idea of handy things to keep around:

- Cooking oil (canola or olive is good)
- Soy sauce or tamari
- Spices: salt and pepper, vegetable seasoning blend, onion powder, garlic powder
- Vegetarian broth mix or bouillon
- Herbal tea
- Honey, maple syrup, or barley malt for sweetening
- Breads: bagels, pitas, English muffins, tortillas, crackers
- Breakfast cereal or instant oatmeal
- Canned beans: refried or whole
- Bottled salsa
- Ramen noodles (get the kind with veggie broth at a natural foods store)
- Macaroni, couscous, instant brown rice, and other fast-cooking grains
- Peanut butter and jelly
- Bananas or apples
- Dried fruit and nuts
- Small boxes of soymilk
- Juice
- Aseptic packaged tofu (doesn't need refrigeration until after it's been opened)

In your mini-fridge:

- A small box or bag of frozen green peas, corn kernels, chopped broccoli, or vegetable blend (if you don't have a big enough freezer section, you can store it in the refrigerator and use in a few days' time)
- Soy or dairy cheese (if you're not vegan, cottage cheese is a handy thing to mix in with cooked noodles and veggies, and soy or dairy parmesan cheese makes everything taste better)

Helpful tools to have on hand:

- A small pot, wooden spoon, spatula, colander or strainer, a big mug ("One you can drink tea or eat soup in," notes Tovah), eating utensils, plate, small baking pan (like a 9-inch square brownie-type pan), lidded plastic containers to store leftovers

If you break out of the dorm scene and head out into your own apartment or shared house, you'll have even more cooking options. Equipped with your own kitchen and recipes, your only limitations will be your budget and your imagination. Mark shares a house with friends at Colorado College. He likes to make burritos using just about anything as a filling: leftover fried rice, thick lentil soup, canned refried beans. Think about how you and your roommates eat—or would like to eat—and look for ways to make it easier. Mark and his housemates pooled their resources to buy an electric rice cooker. "It's good to keep cooked rice in the fridge," he says. "The rice cooker is really nice because we can steam things in it, too."

Whatever your living and dining situation is while you're away at college, remember to enjoy yourself. "Going to college was the second time I went away from home, and both times I worried too much ahead of time about how I was going to manage eating," says Joey. "But you'll always find something that works." It might take a while to figure out what works, what's cheapest, what tastes best, what fills you up—but you will. There are too many other things to think about at school. The food part should be fun.

GLOSSARY
OF
BASIC COOKING TERMS
AND UNUSUAL FOODS

Basic Cooking Terms

Bake: To cook something inside of the oven. Make sure that you *preheat* the oven: turn the oven to the desired temperature and let it heat up before putting in the food.

Boil: To heat a liquid on the stovetop until bubbles break out on the surface. To boil a solid food (like a potato) means to cook the food in boiling water.

Broil: You do this by putting food in the broiler part of the oven, where the heat source is on top of the food. Make sure to set the oven to "broil."

Chop: To cut vegetables into smaller pieces. You can *finely* chop something into very small pieces or *coarsely* chop something into large pieces. To *dice* or *cube* something simply means to chop it into symmetrical, square pieces.

Grill: You know, like on a barbecue.

Puree: To process something into a pulp. You puree foods in a blender or food processor.

Sauté: To cook in a little bit of oil or other liquid over medium heat in a skillet or other pan on the stovetop.

Knife Know-how

A good knife makes chopping vegetables a lot easier. Your parents probably have a decent knife or two in the kitchen. A 10-inch chef's knife is a good all-around knife that you can use for most chopping and slicing. A smaller knife is helpful for little jobs.

You should hold your knife firmly in your cutting hand, but don't squeeze the grip so tightly that your hand hurts. Use your other hand to hold the food you are cutting, curving your fingers under as you chop or slice. (This protects your fingertips.) When chopping something into very fine pieces, some people place their non-cutting hand over the top of the blade (with fingers extended) to help control the blade. It's okay to work slowly at first; the most important thing is to pay attention and be safe. Practice cutting easy things first, like green leafy vegetables, before moving on to more challenging things, like tough root vegetables and winter squash.

Simmer: To simmer a liquid, first bring it to a boil, then turn the heat down and let it cook at a steady little roll. (That little roll is the simmer part.) Simmering gives a chance for flavors to combine and ingredients to cook through.

Steam: To cook foods by placing them over a source of boiling or simmering water—like in a steamer basket. Make sure a lid is on to trap the steam; that's what cooks the food.

Stir-fry: Sort of like sautéing, but in a really hot pan and with faster, more constant stirring.

Unusual Foods

Egg Replacer: A pre-made powdered mix of ingredients that takes the place of eggs in baked goods. Available in natural foods stores.

Miso (pronounced MEE-soh): A concentrated, flavorful paste made from fermented soybeans. It adds a salty, savory flavor to soups, sauces, gravies, and spreads. It comes in different varieties, from light and mellow to dark and very salty. Add miso to your recipes at the end of cooking time and don't boil it; boiling destroys some of miso's nutritional value.

Nutritional Yeast: This is different from the yeast that makes bread rise. Nutritional yeast comes in flake or powdered form and has a golden color and a sort of cheeselike taste. People who don't eat cheese like to keep it around to add to recipes or to sprinkle on pasta dishes instead of parmesan cheese. Available at natural foods stores.

Seitan (pronounced SAY-tan): Seitan is a very meatlike food that's made from wheat flour. Depending on the seasonings, it can take the place of chicken, turkey, beef, or just about anything else. You can buy it in the refrigerated or frozen section of the natural foods store. Try it in Sweet and Spicy Seitan Fajitas (page 74).

Soy Cheese: You can use soy cheese the way you would dairy cheese. Soy cheese doesn't melt quite the same as cow's milk cheese, and it tastes a bit different, but it fills in if you want that cheeselike quality. (Almond cheese is available, too.) Note: most soy cheese contains a small amount of casein, a milk protein, to help it melt.

Soymilk and Other Milk Alternatives: You can use soymilk just as you would cow's milk: over cereal, in cooking and baking, or by the glass. You can find it at natural foods stores and in many supermarkets. Make sure to look for soymilk that is fortified with calcium and vitamin D. Rice milk, almond milk, and oat milk are also available. (By the way, if you want to find a recycling program that accepts soymilk or juice boxes—they're not taken at most recycling places—call the Aseptic Packaging Council at [800] 277-8088.)

Tamari (pronounced ta-MAR-ee): A natural soy sauce brewed using a traditional Japanese method, resulting in a more complex flavor than regular soy sauce. Available in natural foods stores and Asian groceries.

What Kind of Oil to Use?

*Many recipes in this book call for **vegetable oil**. That's a general term that includes canola oil, corn oil, safflower oil, sunflower oil, soybean oil, and others. You can use any of these in your cooking. Some recipes call specifically for **olive oil**, which has a richer taste. It's excellent in pasta, salads, and main dishes, but it's not so good in sweet things. (Note that oils that are high in polyunsaturated fats and monosaturated fats, such as canola oil and olive oil, are believed to be better for you than others containing more saturated fats.)*

Tempeh (pronounced TEM-pay): Tempeh is a dense patty made from soybeans. It can be made into sandwiches, skewered on shish kebabs, or cubed into stir-fries. Grated into sauces or other recipes, it seems very meatlike (see Sloppy Joes, page 55). Tempeh soaks up the flavor of whatever you cook it with. You can find it at natural foods stores or Asian groceries.

Textured Vegetable Protein, or TVP®: TVP is made from soy flour and comes in granules, flakes, or chunks. When you add boiling water and let it moisten, it becomes very meat-like. Try TVP in the Create-Your-Own Veggie Burger, page 56. Available at natural foods stores or from the Mail Order Catalog, P.O. Box 180, Summertown, TN 38483; (800) 695-2241; www.healthy-eating.com.

Tofu (pronounced TOE-foo): Tofu (sometimes called bean curd) is made from soybeans in a process similar to the way that cheese is made from milk. By itself, tofu doesn't taste like much (although I love it plain), but it picks up the flavor of whatever you cook it with. Tofu is rich in protein, iron, and calcium, if you select tofu that was made with calcium sulfate or calcium chloride (two mineral salts).

Tofu Tips

There are different kinds of tofu, and each works best in certain kinds of recipes.

*   **Extra-firm** or **firm** *tofu is great cubed in stir-fries and stews, or sliced, seasoned, and baked, broiled, or sautéed for sandwiches (try Seasoned Tofu Slices, page 31, or Sesame Tofu Triangles, page 32). You can change the texture to a meatier, chewier consistency by freezing and thawing it—good for crumbling into chili and sauces.* **Soft** *and* **silken** *types of tofu are best in smoothies, dips, sauces, dressings, puddings, and pies. (Chocolate Coma Pie, page 151, will make a tofu convert out of anyone.) You can also substitute silken tofu for eggs in some baked goods.*

*   For the best texture, press the water out of firm tofu before using it in recipes. If you're going to cube or slice tofu, use this method: Put the tofu in a large colander in the sink, and place a saucepan of water on top of it. Leave the tofu while you prepare other ingredients; the weight of the filled pan will press the water out of the tofu. If you're going to crumble the tofu, simply wrap the tofu in a towel and press or wring the water out.*

*   Tofu comes either packed in water and refrigerated (the package is often sealed with a clear plastic top) or in aseptic packages that don't need to be refrigerated until you open them. Store any opened and unused tofu in the refrigerator. Water-packed tofu keeps for about a week if you store it in water and change the water daily. Store unused aseptic-packed tofu in an airtight container for about 3 days.*

INDEX